Dear Bill,

A Dove
Among Eagles

How the Sister of One Paratrooper Changed the Lives of Tens of Thousands in Vietnam and Beyond

Thank you for your service
we appreciate all you've
done

hugs

Linda

Praise for A Dove Among Eagles

"Linda Patterson reminded me what America is all about ... people taking care of people, giving without expectation of receiving. When I commanded 1st Brigade 'Bastogne' of the 101st Airborne Division in Iraq, 2003-2004, she connected nearly all 16 of our Companies in the Brigade to communities across America. Through her, so many of our Soldiers received support and encouragement from Americans they'd never met. This is powerful — it gives young Soldiers confidence in their mission and purpose. And that's why, when we returned from that first year in Iraq, we made her an Honorary Member of the Brigade, the same unit of the 101st Airborne Division in which her brother and her husband had served in Vietnam. Years later, in San Mateo, California, I had the privilege to participate in the 50th Anniversary of the return of Joe's Company from Vietnam with several of the surviving Veterans from that time. What an amazing experience! I met so many terrific Veterans and could see first-hand the relationship between them and Linda and Steve. What struck me most, however, were the people of San Mateo ... the generosity and the sincere appreciation of the Veterans. Honestly, the flag-waving and small-town Americana were not what I'd expected from a city on America's West Coast. Boy, was I wrong! Because of Linda Patterson, I gained a whole new appreciation for my own country."

Lieutenant General Ben Hodges, U.S. Army, Retired

"Fifty years ago, in a combat zone, in a war with Vietnam (1968), l, Captain Julius Johnson, Company Commander of A Company, 1st Battalion, 327th Infantry Regiment, 101st Airborne Division, was approached by one of my Soldiers, Sergeant Joe Artavia, with a request to authenticate a Company Roster. This Roster was to be used by SGT Artavia's sister, Linda, to convince a community, San Mateo, CA, to provide moral support to the Airborne Paratroopers of our unit. The United States of America had strong sentiments against the war in Vietnam, and support for the Soldiers fighting was mixed. It would be difficult to convince a community, but she succeeded, and in March 1968 our unit was adopted. This began unwavering support to our Soldiers as they pursued a More Perfect Union. Linda Patterson's support for our Division over the past 50 years is unprecedented. The compensation for Mrs. Patterson, as the spiritual voice of the Soldiers to the community, has been the loyalty and love shared by the Soldiers of the 101st Airborne Division, and a grateful nation. Jon Meacham, in his book, *The Soul of America*, captures Mrs. Patterson's flight through destiny and states, 'To know what has come before is to be armed against despair. If the men and women of the past, with all of their flaws and limitations and ambitions and appetites, could press on through ignorance and superstition, racism, and sexism, selfishness and greed, to create a freer, stronger nation, then perhaps we too can fight wrongs and take another step toward that most enchanting and elusive of destinations, A More Perfect Union.' Mrs. Patterson's travel through time has been eventful and historical. She is truly 'Above the Rest!'"

Brigadier General Julius F. Johnson, U.S. Army, Retired

"The terrorist attacks of 9/11 and the following war on terror have brought about a whole new level of support for America's fighting men and women. As a retired Army Chief Warrant Officer and Iraq war Veteran, I have been the benefactor of much love and support from so many people that I've lost count. I have also witnessed something very special, yet so long overdue ... a new appreciation and sincere gratitude for our Vietnam Veterans. Here, in Linda's new book *A Dove Among Eagles*, you will find words that tell a story all Americans, young and old, need to read. Linda gives us an inside look to so much raw history through the lens of her own eyes. How incredibly enriched we are to have this new book in our hands! Read it, share it, and talk about it. Job well done, Linda. I salute you!"

Robert "Bo" Brabo, Chief Warrant Officer 3, U.S. Army, Retired

Author of *From the Battlefield to the White House to the Boardroom*, and Vice President of Human Resources at The National Spine & Pain Centers

"I am thrilled beyond words at the publishing of a book about Linda Patterson's story — about her brother Joe Artavia and the good that can come from loss. I consider Linda to be the matriarch of the 1st Brigade of the 101st Airborne Division. She has done more than anyone else to connect our military to the citizenry whom we serve, and it all started with a letter from SGT Joe Artavia over 50 years ago. Driven by a passion to care for her Screaming Eagles, Linda has dedicated her life to ensuring that our Soldiers' morale soars 'higher than the clouds.' Linda's story is uniquely American — overcoming all odds to form a partnership between community and military that was unheard of in 1968 ... a partnership that today serves as the example for our entire Armed Forces. Her work extends beyond community relations to connect us to our Veterans as well. Ms. Linda Patterson will always hold a special place in the history of the 101st Airborne Division, and I am personally grateful for all she has done to help us maintain that strong bond between today's servicemembers and our Veterans who came before us. Commanders come and go, but Linda has been an active source of continuity, always reaching out and always connecting."

Colonel Derek K. Thomson, U.S. Army

"On the morning of 9/11/2001 — a day of infamy — I joined a line of somber Americans to order coffee at the Starbucks in Pacific Palisades, California. I noticed a middle-aged woman wearing a U.S. Army fatigue jacket with a 'Screaming Eagles' patch on it, of the storied 101st Airborne Division. I immediately introduced myself to her and asked how she got that jacket. Although I was now a UCLA neurologist, I had been a Soldier in 1969, attached to the 101st in Vietnam. She told me she was Linda Patterson and we sat down at a table to talk. Her younger brother, Sergeant Joe Artavia, Linda told me, was an infantryman killed in action, and had been the inspiration for the founding of America Supporting Americans. Her husband of many years, Steve, had been Joe's platoon leader, and they both knew that America would be at war again, and ASA would be reactivated to support a new generation of young Americans facing danger far from home. Without hesitation, she asked me, 'Doctor Spooner, would you be willing to help?' That moment changed my life — for here was a woman, a healer of the wounds of war, willing to relive her own pain, to assuage the loneliness of the trooper in the field of battle. This is her story."

Joseph W. Spooner, MD

Vietnam Veteran, ASA Board Member (Poway, California)

"I am thankful to Linda for sharing what I know are painful memories for her. And what an awesome job she's done to keep her brother's memory alive by turning his loss into support for the tens of thousands of Soldiers who've benefited from her inspiration. Linda Patterson is a blessing."

Libby Graham Baker

ASA Liaison Leader, Crescent Springs, Kentucky

"I met Linda Patterson while commanding Soldiers in the Army's 101st Airborne Division. Each year, we would invite back our Vietnam Veterans for a reunion — a time I cherished, meeting the grizzly, old war-torn warriors, *Screaming Eagles*, who were the trailblazers of the unit I now commanded. Among them? A dove. Linda. Like the actual bird, she is a symbol of peace. Linda's beauty, her presence and her story caught my attention and the attention of so many others. Since that first day, I've treasured our friendship and admired her love of country, of Soldiers, of her husband Steve and of her brother Sergeant Joe Artavia, who paid the ultimate sacrifice in Vietnam in 1968. Take flight with the Dove, Linda Patterson, in this wonderful book. I've read countless books on war and have experienced its effects personally and there is nothing quite like this magnificent story, decades in the making, captured so eloquently in this masterpiece. Few understand service and sacrifice like Linda Patterson. In honor of her brother's final wish, to raise the morale of his unit and to keep his memory and the memory of all the fallen alive, she continues to serve. As the President of America Supporting Americans, she leads a movement of citizens supporting deployed service members and urging cities across our country to adopt military units. Now you can enjoy Linda's presence and her selflessness in yet another fitting tribute to her brother Joe in this captivating saga of tragedy, triumph, servitude and love, *A Dove Among Eagles*."

Colonel Rob Campbell, U.S. Army, Retired

Author of the books *At Ease: Enjoying the Freedom You Fought For — A Soldier's Story and Perspectives on the Journey to an Encore Life and Career*, and *It's Personal, Not Personnel: Leadership Lessons for the Battlefield and the Boardroom*

"Linda Patterson is an inspiration ... a force of sheer will and a relentless pursuit of support for our military."

Nancy Taylor

ASA Liaison Leader and former teacher for Beechwood Elementary School, Adopted City Fort Mitchell, Kentucky

"*A Dove Among Eagles* describes Linda Patterson's efforts to let our troops know they are not forgotten. While her efforts and experiences are documented and historical, they are also deeply personal. Just ask the troops she helped about her true impact during their time in country and for many years after."

Jim Reynolds, Petty Officer, 2nd Class, U.S. Navy, In-Country, 1968

"As I sit here, once again deployed in support of our country, I think back to other deployments where America Supporting Americans (ASA) and Linda Patterson had such a profound impact on the morale of the units I have commanded. For 15 years, with the help of ASA, units I have commanded have been supported from home while defending our nation. This book will give you a small glimpse into Linda's life and how her love for this country and those who defend it came to be. Linda Patterson's dedication to this country and the military that defends its freedoms are absolutely second to none."

Colonel Brandon Teague, U.S. Army

"I am one of the first, original Adopted Sons of A Company 1st 327th Infantry Regiment of the 101st Airborne Division — the first and only unit to be adopted by an American City, San Mateo, California, during the Vietnam War. I have lived and personally experienced what it means to have complete strangers back home step up and adopt, support, care for and write to deployed Soldiers when their morale is so down and in the dumpster! I will never forget Linda's grace, courage, humility, and true sincerity as she met and greeted each and every one of us as her own brothers! It was a surreal moment in the history of the Company! We were like a bunch of kids who hadn't seen their older sister in years!!! We were truly blessed by God when he placed SGT Joe Artavia in our ranks. Joe blessed us with his big sister, who in turn blessed us with the great citizens of a really great 'little' town called San Mateo, California. They were true

Americans who stepped up and adopted and supported their combat sons during the most turbulent of times in our country's history (when that was not the most popular thing to be doing). They brought us up out of the ashes and gave us back our humanity. They 'Raised Our Morale as High as the Clouds!'"

Sergeant Bill Smith, U.S. Army, Retired

AKA Rick Smith, AKA "Wild Bill," A Company, 1st Battalion, 327th Infantry Regiment, 101st Airborne Division, Vietnam, 1968-1969

"My relationship with the 101st Screaming Eagles began 51 years ago when I was in 8th grade and student body president of St. Gregory School in San Mateo. I was deeply moved by Linda Patterson's appeal to the city to adopt the 101st Airborne Division and I helped organize a letter-writing campaign to the soldiers. Fast forward 42 years and I found myself once again proudly supporting our troops while serving as Mayor and a Council Member for the great City of San Mateo.

A Dove Among Eagles is more than the story of Linda's lifelong commitment to our troops. It is an incredible love story on multiple levels: a sister's deep love for her adored kid brother; a courageous journey to a Vietnam war zone where — amidst the tragedy of her brother's death — she finds the love of her life; and a woman's passionate patriotism and deep love for our troops, which has become her steadfast mission of service for more than 50 years. Linda's candid, often heart-wrenching story will inspire you, move you to tears as well laughter, and take you on a memorable journey of soul-searching reflection. I couldn't put it down!"

Maureen Freschet

Former Mayor and Council Member, City of San Mateo, California

"I am so proud of my dear friend, Linda Patterson, and thrilled that her dream to write her story has become a reality!!! When our cities became part of the ASA program, we also become part of the 'Top Guns' family based in Fort Campbell, Kentucky. ASA is a special gift that has connected our military heroes and their families with communities throughout the country and builds memories that will last a lifetime. ASA and our military connections are attributable to the love, devotion, courage and persistence of Linda Patterson."

Julie Schuler

ASA Co-Liaison, Villa Hills, Kentucky

"Linda's story demonstrates how she leads with her heart first, with vision, tenacity, courage, and creativity. Her commitment is inspirational and shows that one person, with vision and purpose, can truly make a difference. There will forever be a lasting legacy between the City of San Mateo and our adopted unit that grows stronger every day. Her brother Joe — and all of ABU — are San Mateo's sons and daughters, and Linda is our cool aunt who does crazy things that, afterward, make everyone smack their forehead and go 'of course!' She sets the bar for crazy as brilliant — such as when she flew to Vietnam to deliver medallions in the jungle to our adopted sons in the middle of the war. Linda is the lady with a heart who ensured this City had a heart when it needed to."

Patrice M. Olds

City Clerk, City of San Mateo, California

A Dove Among Eagles

How the Sister of One Paratrooper
Changed the Lives of Tens of
Thousands in Vietnam and Beyond

Linda Patterson

With a foreword by Colonel Rob Campbell, U.S. Army, Retired,
Former 1st Brigade Commander, 101st Airborne Division

Silver
Linings
MEDIA

Editing by:
Kate Colbert

Cover design and typesetting by:
Courtney Hudson

First edition, January 2020

ISBN: 978-1-948238-22-9

Library of Congress Control Number: 2019916395

Created in the United States of America

Dedication

For Joe ...

What do you say about a kid brother who was taken from you because of War, but who was not silenced? *A Dove Among Eagles* gave him back his voice.

Table of Contents

Foreword

By Colonel Rob Campbell, U.S. Army, Retired

When the 101st Airborne Division was founded in 1942, its first commander, Major General William C. Lee remarked, "We have no history, but we have a rendezvous with destiny." This statement, still spoken and sung in chorus at Fort Campbell, Kentucky, headquarters of the 101st, remains a deep belief of the men and women who serve there. These Soldiers — the Screaming Eagles —wear on their shoulder one of the most recognizable emblems of the American military, the eagle with the inscription Airborne above it, in homage to their Civil War-era mascot, the bald eagle. This patch represents a rich résumé of combat from the drop zones of Normandy, to the frozen forests of Bastogne, Belgium, to Vietnam, Iraq and Afghanistan.

I would have my own rendezvous with destiny in 2013 when the Army selected me to command the 1st Brigade of the 101st Airborne Division. There I would meet Linda Patterson and her husband Steve. My brigade had a long history of service in Vietnam, leading the division there in 1965 and fighting for more than seven years. Annually after the end of the war, the Veterans of this conflict would reunite at Fort Campbell, regale their stories of battle and interact with the brigade's current members. I have attended several of these reunions and cherished these times, meeting legendary Vietnam-era Screaming Eagles, trailblazers of the unit I now commanded.

I'd been around plenty of older Veterans before, but this group was different. Linda made it so. It was a stunning yet beautiful contrast — these men, hardened by combat, living treasures of war, and this dove, a symbol of peace, Linda Patterson. Linda's beauty, her presence and her story caught my attention and the attention of so many others. Since the very first day I met her, I've treasured our friendship and admired her love of country, of Soldiers, of her husband Steve and of her brother, Sergeant Joseph ("Joe") Artavia, who paid the ultimate sacrifice in Vietnam in 1968.

Though I've lost many friends and Soldiers in my years in combat, I never lost a family member in such a way. I've never walked in Linda's shoes. I've telephoned the mothers of Soldiers killed, to offer what comfort I could. I've handed folded American flags to widows as a final thank you from a grateful nation, but I have always wondered how they handle such grief. I know there are numerous studies about such grief and methods for approaching such a tragedy, but despite my curiosity, I haven't read a single one. In truth, I think I'd prefer not to know. It must be — and I believe should be — a very personal and private journey, traveled in a way that gives solace to those left behind.

I know enough to understand that the wounds of grief never really heal. There is no true closure, only consolation, in whatever form, as one attempts to cope with such a loss. We honor the fallen by living good lives and Linda is a fine example of that. I won't speak for her, but I suspect this book is akin to another bandage she can place on her forever-fractured heart. It is yet another tribute among all her good deeds to a brother she loved.

Sergeant Joe Artavia died gloriously on the field of battle. He was taken from Linda, yet gave her so much. I know Joe only as a paratrooper — a Screaming Eagle — but I know he would be tremendously proud of his sis. Have a look at his official Army photo and I believe you can see this pride — pride in being a paratrooper, pride in his sister for all she has done and continues to do.

Joe's final wish, to raise the morale of his unit, lives through Linda. Like a fellow warrior on the field of battle, Linda grabbed the flag and continues the mission as a "fighter for the good." As the president of America Supporting Americans, she serves a new band of brothers and sisters, each one brought to her by Joe. She remains "on the trail," leading a movement of citizens supporting deployed service members and urging cities across our country to adopt military units. With every care package and letter of love and support from home, Joe's legacy lives. And now, Joe's legacy continues to live in the pages of this book.

A Dove Among Eagles is a book like no other. Turn the pages and experience your own rendezvous with destiny. Take flight with the dove, Linda Patterson, back to the turbulent 1960s, to the streets and city hall of San Mateo, California, to the firebases of Vietnam and to modern-day Fort Campbell, Kentucky. I've read countless books on war and experienced its effects personally. This book and story of war is in a class by itself, decades in the making, captured so eloquently in this masterpiece. You'll laugh, cry, cheer and even sing along to the epic songs of the era as Linda unveils her story and pays tribute to her brother, her husband Steve and those who serve their country.

Few understand service and sacrifice like Linda Patterson. Experience Linda's presence, bravery and her selflessness in yet another fitting tribute to her brother Joe in this captivating saga of tragedy, triumph, servitude and love ... *A Dove Among Eagles*.

Colonel Rob Campbell, U.S. Army, Retired

Author of the books *At Ease: Enjoying the Freedom You Fought For — A Soldier's Story and Perspectives on the Journey to an Encore Life and Career*, and *It's Personal, Not Personnel: Leadership Lessons for the Battlefield and the Boardroom*

Introduction

A Special Note to Readers from the Author's Husband, Steve Patterson

He Ain't Heavy, He's My Brother

Christmas 1968

All you have to do is look at photographs of Linda as a child. That beautiful face has stayed with her for her entire life. When I look at those childhood pictures, I see something that goes beyond outward beauty. That sweet smile tells me this is someone

Linda's First Communion, with her grandmother

who has always been destined to affect the lives of others. There was a moment, I believe, when this destiny was realized.

Linda had waited days for the men to be brought in from jungle operations. On Christmas Eve Day, they finally arrived. Standing there in formation, they showed her what few civilians would ever see — the raw look of combat. The men had not had any rest since August and had not had the opportunity to clean up for Linda. They were unshaven, emaciated, wearing jungle fatigue uniforms they had been wearing for months. In their eyes, a collective blank stare. Linda looked upon them with shock. When I glanced at her, I saw a tear running down her cheek. It was at that moment that her life's mission was borne. It was also the moment that I fell in love with her.

Linda at age 10, 1951

I've always felt that it was my responsibility to take care of her as best I could for our Brigade, the 101st Airborne Division, and for all our service men and women who have come to love her so deeply.

She is my hero! I suspect that, after you read this book, she'll be your hero too.

Steve Patterson

Former 1st LT and Platoon Leader, A CO. (ABU), 1/327 Infantry Regiment, 101st Airborne Division, 1968, U.S. Army

Prologue

As a girl who had many homes and very little stability growing up, it's perhaps ironic that my life's mission has been about community, hometowns and a deep sense of connection. I've committed more than 50 years to asking communities in the United States to become "hometown sponsors" for different units of the military — first the Army's famed 101st Airborne Division and now units in all branches of service. It's not that I never had a hometown myself; I did ... San Francisco. But during the first 17 years of my life, my mom, brothers and I lived at several addresses. Later, from age 17 to 24, it seemed like I moved from city to city, wherever the wind blew me.

When people learn about my story, they say I should write a book, to share with the world the promise I made in my 20s to my middle brother Joe. Over the past 50 years, I have collected and shared memories ... doing everything but writing a book. I've been making short notes from my rusty memory; I've been interviewed by the news media; I've appeared on local and national TV; and my husband, Steve, and I have even been in a documentary film. So I guess there has always been a book in the works.

Eventually, I asked a dear friend to consult with me, to help and inspire me. Reluctantly he said yes, that he would help, "but only" ... only if I told the unvarnished truth. Because there is already too much boring, overly edited, politically correct fluff about the Vietnam War Era and its aftermath. Those were "crazy times." And this is a straightforward, honest book. I wrote in one of my scrapbooks that there's "nothing profound about these words written by a young woman ..." And that might be true. But I hope they are words that matter to you and to those you have known, loved, lost or honored.

Throughout *A Dove Among Eagles* are chapter titles and subheadings inspired by popular songs of the 1960s, 1970s and beyond. I hope you find yourself humming or even singing along ... transported to the most memorable moments of our lives. Music can take us back, break or open our hearts, and even help us heal. For a full listing of the songs and artists mentioned in this book, see "Songs and Lyrics: The Music We Lived (and Died) By" on page 181.

Chapter 1

Listen

The time? The 1960s. And we were mired in a period of dissent among the American people. The cause? The Vietnam War. Crazy times, as I have said. Crazy times.

Yet, through all the friction and craziness, there was a deep need for UNITY and, therefore, a unique opportunity to share a message of understanding.

For the first time in our lives, we could look around and sense a "mood" in our country and it was a somber one. Our brothers and cousins in uniform in Vietnam could sense it too — a breakdown of the spirit at home. I found myself among the Silent Majority who believed in our men (boys!) fighting and dying in that War and we were the sad witnesses to the chaos that was happening in our streets. College campuses and city streets were brimming with protestors, whose anti-war messages inevitably sounded less like rally cries to "bring home the troops" and more like indictments of the young servicemen themselves. It was with sadness and anger that we heard news stories about the celebrity who chose to visit the enemy instead of our boys who needed home support. In the line of fire in Vietnam, our Soldiers wondered, *"Do they care?"* We cared.

One City — the City of San Mateo, California — stood steadfast in that care for decades, and this is the unique layer behind this not-so-typical war story. And when it comes to this story, I have a key. It's not golden or silver, and it's not of a size to fit a tiny locket or a large safe. However, it's a key just the same. To me, it's very precious and I hold it near because it is the key to my skeleton closet. I will open it here to allow my readers to peek in and know where I came from and the frame of mind that led me to be a bit carefree and naïve when I was ever so young. As you're about to learn, I lived my own life with no fear of the danger or the consequences. That is, until they drove up to my front door in military uniforms and turned my life upside down.

Mama Was a Rollin' Stone[1]

Although I was born in San Jose, California, I have successfully erased those dreadful memories of my earliest years of life. I remember only being a small child the day my mother, baby brother Johnny and I snuck out of the house to board a Greyhound bus headed to San Francisco. I was only four or five years old, but I remember my mother's fear of my brother's father, Richard, beating her. We were running for our lives, or at least for hers.

It wasn't the first time in my short life that we'd changed homes and male heads of household. My mother had decided to leave my father, Ray, when I was two. She later told me that he was too quiet and boring, and that she needed someone who was more interesting who would smile and make her laugh. Anyway, she moved in with my father's cousin Richard and then, a short time later, my brother Johnny was born. I was very young and assume there must have been good times too, but I only remember the drinking, the screaming and the physical fights. Richard was a mean man who would go to church on Sunday, light a candle, and then come home to beat my mom.

One night, Mom woke me up very early before the sun rose. She told me not to make a sound and that we are going to see Grandma. In the end, I guess her dream of finding someone to make her smile didn't work out so well for her.

> ## Richard was a mean man who would go to church on Sunday, light a candle, and then come home to beat my mom.

Moving in with my grandmother on Alvarado Street in San Francisco introduced us to a life that was quite different. No more crying or yelling. No more watching my mother being abused. My grandmother Rose took care of the three of us until mom found work. Getting settled in at my grandmother's house impeded my enrollment into school that fall, so I was held back six months. In those days, because of the influx of Baby Boomers like me into the school systems, there were what they called "high and low grades" at six-month intervals. Where you were placed (spring or fall semester) was decided by what time of the year you were born. Because I was held back six months, I was just slightly older than the rest in my class, which didn't seem to bother me ... until I got to high school.

While we were living with my grandmother, Mom found a job and soon met John Artavia, who had just gotten out of the Army, having served during World War II (WWII). He was a handsome man who many said looked like the actor Tyrone Power. Mom and John were soon married and we moved to a house on Ashbury Street where my second brother Joe was born. Joey was a New Year's baby, born on January 1, 1949. John Artavia was thrilled that he had a son and, oh my gosh, the sun rose and shined on Joey!

Joe was my kid brother, the middle of two other brothers (Johnny and eventually Eddie), I was seven when Joe was born on New Year's Day. I pretended he was my little doll, having to feed him and change

his diaper. It was every little girl's dream ... a real, live baby doll.
We stayed on Ashbury Street in San Francisco until a couple years
after the birth of Joe, when we moved to Potrero Hill, a blue-collar
neighborhood on Missouri Street. Our apartment was a typical San
Francisco two-story Victorian flat. These flats usually held two families. It was a mixed neighborhood of Italians, Mexicans, Russians and
Slovaks, typical of San Francisco culture. It was great! Now we had
room to play outside. However, being the oldest, I was told it was my
responsibility to look after my brothers as we played. I don't recall it
being much of a burden, though, when I was nine through 12. In fact,
I enjoyed leading my three younger brothers, Joey, Johnny, and my
new little brother Eddie, playing cowboys or war games in empty lots
near my house.

As I said, the
neighborhood was
great, there were
a lot of kids and
we loved spending
our time outdoors.
I remember Mom
sticking her head
out the window
of the two-story
flat we lived in,
calling us in for

Eddie, Grandma Rose and Joey

dinner. Her voice carried across those empty lots and, I have to tell
you, when we heard Mom calling, we stopped what we were doing
and ran home as fast as we could, daring not to be late. My stepfa-
ther, John Artavia, was very strict raising us and we knew better than
to make him wait or make him angry. That said, I must add that of
all of mom's husbands (in all, there were five), he was the only one
who gave us some semblance of "a real family life." Though he was

a tough disciplinarian, I was grateful to him in the long run. It was then, between the ages of five and 14, that the roots of my development began. I loved playing teacher to my brothers on rainy days when we couldn't play outside. I would set up a "classroom" and make them do homework, let them color pictures and I would grade them. We had a "secret club" under the house where we all played. Joey was a toddler when I was 10, but he always wanted to be included in the games I played with Johnny and with my friends. I was very much a tom boy because I was surrounded by brothers and I have to admit I liked being the boss. I taught Joey how to skate and I took him trick-or-treating. He was like a puppy, following me everywhere I went. As kids, we lived near a big open lot with tall grass, which made a perfect place for us to have our war games, as kids did in those days. Pulling up grass bombs and throwing them at the bad guys (i.e., the neighbor kids). We took prisoners and knew the script from the John Wayne movies we watched. No bikes where allowed because A) we couldn't afford them and B) we lived on steep hills. So we improvised with street kid roller coasters (flat boards with ball-bearing skate wheels), using a rope to guide us and our feet as brakes. I read a lot of comic books and would tell stories to Joey, Johnny and Eddie.

Born to Be a Warrior

As a little kid, Joey was tough, always wanted to be the Captain while playing our war games and I would scold him and tell him he was too young and had to be my sergeant, which he would agree to.

I recall hearing that, after I had already moved out of the house, some tough Mission Street kids had stolen my brother Eddie's paper-route money. Hearing this, Joe waited for them the next time they approached Eddie. He stood up to them with fist clenched, prepared to defend his little brother. The cowards ran off because they knew

Joe meant business. He was probably 10 years old then. Joe was a fighter, but only for the good. Once on a paper route of his own, tossing papers from the window of a truck, the truck's driver deliberately ran over a small baby bird in the street, thinking it was funny. Although they were miles from home in the early morning hours, Joe was furious, jumped out of the truck and walked the rest of the way home, refusing to get back in the truck with that jerk.

Joe was a fighter, but only for the good.

Mom worked hard to provide the best care for us she could. However, she was deeply flawed. First of all, how should I put this? I mean, she married five different men! I might add, though, that she was consistent. She had a knack for marrying the same type of person over and over. She seemed to be, more or less, in love with being in love. Back in the day, couples didn't live together if they weren't legally married. So Mom feared that people would talk if she lived with a man who wasn't her husband (as if they didn't talk behind her back about her marrying over and over again!). But serial matrimony wasn't her worst flaw; her worst flaw was that she drank. She had a serious drinking problem and it became worse as I grew older. I hated to see her that way. She would always become mean and say very hurtful things. Mom drank more heavily than John Artavia and, as a result, they eventually divorced.

The new man in my mom's life after separating from Joey's dad John was named Richard (yes, another Richard, but not the same Richard who was my first brother Johnny's dad). This new Richard became a drinking partner for Mom. In fact, I think she met him at the corner bar. Although they would only drink (or "party," as we all called it) during the weekends, I hated being around her. My brothers, thankfully, were too young to understand.

There were a lot of "father figures" in our lives, but not a lot of connection with my real dad, Ray. He lived with his new family in Menlo Park, and I saw little of him except during summer vacations. So it was my grandmother — who mercifully lived with us for much of my childhood — who I looked to for advice and nurturing. My grandmother was like a mother to me — always inspiring me to better myself and urging me to learn more from my surroundings and the company I kept. She encouraged me to reach for the sky, and not to shed so many tears (she would tell me to save my tears for her when she passes). My grandmother was the tower of strength I looked up to as a child. She had a sixth-grade education due to a childhood illness that took her out of school, yet she learned a trade and worked her way up to holding top jobs as an alteration seamstress in some of the finest San Francisco department stores: City of Paris, White House, and I. Magnin. She had even survived the 1906 San Francisco earthquake.

My grandmother was the tower of strength I looked up to as a child.

I loved listening to her stories. She sheltered us kids as much as she could from the dysfunctional family of divorces and alcoholism. It's one thing when your father drinks, but watching your mother drink and fall and drink some more ... it tarnishes your childhood memories even more. And if you're anything like me, all you can do is wait for the escape and take an oath that you will never be like that when you grow up.

That doesn't mean you stop loving your mother; I always loved my mother. She was beautiful and a totally different (good, wonderful) person when she didn't drink. Looking back, I realize she was not a happy woman and I know she had many regrets about always putting her husbands before her children. Somehow, I'll never forget her reasoning for that: "Linda, someday you'll leave me, and he won't." (She was right, of course. "He" never left her. She did all the leaving.) I promised myself that I would never say something like that to my own children — never make them feel guilty for the natural progression of growing up and moving away.

When I turned 14, it was like letting the horse out of the barn. I ran.

I was able to convince my grandmother to move out with me and for us to get our own apartment, leaving my younger brothers behind. We didn't move far, just maybe a few blocks down the hill. Grandma and I found a cute little apartment, which was just perfect for us. When I would visit my mom, my brothers would run up to the door, excited to see me. They'd scream, "Linda's here, Linda's here!" I don't know why they got so excited, but they did, every time they saw me. Living with my grandmother was great, but she most certainly was not capable of handling a teenage girl going on 15. With my newfound freedom, I went to school, hung out with my girlfriends and thought of boys 24/7. No longer having my strict stepdad to enforce that I complete my homework, and without any guidance, I dreamed of the day I could quit school, get a fantastic job, marry and have kids. That was pretty much the dream in those days, at least for my friends and me. So I did!

Though I had left the nest to start my own life, my little brothers still figured largely into my life. As for Joe, whose life's story is the inspiration for this book, I loved him like crazy but he and I had our arguments, as all siblings do. Just before he left for boot camp, he asked to borrow my car to spend the day with his friends. "OK," I said, "but only in town. Don't leave San Francisco." Later I found out he took my car to Disneyland and got a parking ticket. Was I angry? Yes, but I regret that burst of anger to my little brother before he went off to boot camp.

Joe had a great singing voice and, in high school, he performed in a school band. It was like a spotlight club during high school assemblies. My favorite memories of him singing include "Town Without Pity"[2] and his version of "The Impossible Dream."[3] Joe's high school buddy Patrick joined the Army with him, and said he believed Joe could someday have his own band because his voice was that good. We all had some quality time together before the Army sent him to Vietnam. While I was living in Sacramento, we went horseback riding together, where he told me about a girl he really cared for. They made plans to marry after Vietnam. While he was in boot camp at Fort Ord, he received his "Dear John" letter from her. Years later, his Army buddy told me that he and Joe had gone AWOL one weekend to try to talk with her ... to win her back. They both got KP duty when they returned to the base. He received another, final Dear John from her while in Vietnam.

Chapter 2
Dream On[4]

> There is something about being a free young woman
> living on her own in a city like San Francisco.

There is something about being a free young woman living on her own in a city like San Francisco.

For me, moving out of the house at 14 wasn't enough. At 16, while still in high school, I wanted to live on my own. So I got a part-time job and found a cheap apartment on Fell Street in the Haight-Asbury district, close to Poly (Polytechnic High School). I think it was seeing my friends graduate ahead of me that made me want to quit. That whole Baby Boomer "low and high grades" thing left me six months behind many of my friends, and I wanted to fast-track my experience to adulthood. Foolishly, I quit school when I was 17. I told myself that I was well prepared. After all, I had been working at the Haight Theater for minimum wage as an usherette since I was 16 and trying to keep up with school. Realizing I needed more money, I looked for a second job to help make ends meet. That's when I found my first real job at a bank in the Financial District of San Francisco. Of course, I lied about graduating from high school. I may not have had the credentials but, by my way of thinking, if I wasn't 100% book smart, I was 100% street smart. I was hired as a file clerk. This was so cool.

I got to dress like a businesswoman and act like an adult. Did I need
a higher education? I think not! I kept remembering my grandmother's words: "Listen and learn along the way, Linda, and always
associate with people in upper levels. Watch and learn!!"

If I wasn't 100% book smart, I was 100% street smart.

With all due respect to listening and learning in grown-up office
jobs, the best job for a 17-year-old was in the movie theatres. What
a fantastic job that was! I was getting paid to watch all the movies of
the '50s and early '60s: like *A Summer Place, Cat on a Hot Tin Roof,
Some Like It Hot, The Fly,* and James Bond in *Dr. No* and *From Russia
With Love.* For those of you who don't know about movie ushers (and
those of you who have forgotten), allow me to tell you what it was like
back in the day. We were gallant men and women who escorted you
to your seats at the movies. But that was at a time when movie ushers
did much more than tear tickets and sweep up spilled popcorn; we
kept an eye out for miscreants attempting to sneak in without paying,
offered a helpful elbow to women walking down the steeply inclined
aisle in high-heeled shoes, and were quick to "Shhh" to folks who
talked during the movie.

Ushers carried small flashlights to guide patrons who arrived after
the movie had started and we were also the ones who maintained
order when the film broke and the audience grew ornery. Of course,
cell phones hadn't yet been invented, so doctors or parents who'd left
youngsters home with a babysitter often mentioned such to the usher
as they were seated, so we'd be able to find them during the show
if an emergency phone call was received for them at the box office.
Those were good times.

I remember thinking, "Gee, this job held some amount of authority!"
Ha! Remember, folks, this was a 17-year-old girl thinking.

The pinnacle of my usherette career was when I was employed by Paramount & Golden Gate Theaters on Market Street at the princely sum of $1.50 an hour! That's when I first met Al Giese. He too came from a dysfunctional family and throughout his life could not get past that. Early on, he was so nice and I liked the attention he showered on me. I was 18 and he was 17 (Al seemed older than his years). We took our breaks together at the coffee shop across the street and he would come to my apartment in the evenings. We both had a lot in common, having left home as teenagers, and both coming from broken homes with alcoholic parents. We sort of hit it off right away and, after only a few weeks, Al asked me to marry him. Perhaps I had seen too many romantic movies so, against my best friend's wishes, I said yes. My friend's advice, that "He's not the one for you Linda," went unheeded. Al and I both longed to have a home and family, so off we drove to Reno, Nevada, to be married.

Adrift

My friend had been right ... Al wasn't the one for me. What we both found, though not love, was companionship and acceptance of one another for almost seven years. Early in the marriage, I knew I had made a mistake by marrying him but the greater fear — greater than staying in the wrong marriage — was that I was following my mother's pattern. For that reason, I was determined that I had to try to make it work. I loved my mother, but I hated her failures: drinking and men. I so wanted a different life for my kids and me. Al had a good heart and tried, but there was the absence of love on my part. We had made the classic mistake. Two lost souls thrown together for all the wrong reasons, too young and imperfectly matched.

After having my beautiful baby boy Craig, I became pregnant again. I quit both of my jobs (at the bank and the theater) and we packed up and left for Oakland, where Al had gotten a job as a jewelry salesman.

Al was a good salesman and a good talker. We found an apartment near Lake Merritt and, shortly afterwards, our daughter Destiny was born at the Oakland County Hospital. (Destiny … now is that a "flower power" name from the '60s or what?) Al was offered a job in a small town, Junction City, Kansas, selling jewelry. He convinced me it would be a good career move for him. So we packed up again, this time as a family of four. We were in Junction City for three months when he lost that job, and we literally had to hitch a ride back home to San Francisco.

I turned 21 on that long ride home and had my first legal drink in Denver. When we got back to San Francisco, we (again) lived with my grandmother for a few weeks then we left for Sacramento. Al got a job as a car salesman, and I found employment with a loan company. Things got tight when Al lost his job again. Is there a pattern developing here? I remember the humiliation of standing in a line at a Catholic church to pick up a couple of bags of donated groceries. I thought of leaving him then, but worried that I would be following my mom's divorce path, so I toughed it out with Al and stayed. Al was kind and loving but we were always in debt. He couldn't seem to hold onto a job for long and he began to drink. It seemed like we never lived in one place for more than a year. The kids were still very young, so I told myself all this moving around didn't hurt them.

Al went to San Francisco by himself to look for work, while I stayed in Sacramento with the kids. We had no money and I couldn't pay the rent. I got so homesick after a couple of weeks of being alone that, in desperation, I packed up my kids and walked to the freeway near our apartment. I left everything behind and, with the kids in tow, hitched a ride back to San Francisco. Lucky for me, soon after walking on the side of that freeway, a car with two young guys stopped and asked me where I was headed. "San Francisco," I said. Talk about the luck of the Irish — they were headed there as well! Boy, was I naïve; I never worried that the kids and I might be headline news the next day. It turned out they had gone to the same high school that I had, Polytechnic. They were nice guys and drove me right up to the front door of my grandmother's apartment. Al was staying with my grandmother while looking for a job, so our little family was reunited. Al soon got another job, this time as a union leader. My grandmother didn't particularly like Al because he drank and couldn't hold a job, but she accepted him. We were able save our money while living with my grandmother and moved to an apartment in South San Francisco.

I Wanna Be an Airborne Ranger, Live a Life of Blood and Danger

My brothers had grown up as fast, as I had, and they desperately wanted out of the house too. At this point, the youngest among us, Eddie, was 13 and stayed home with my mom and her new husband Victor (who turned out to be the man she had always looked for and the love of her life). John and Joey had followed my footsteps in fleeing from home while young. John, my oldest brother, was 15 when he left home in search of his dad, who lived in San Jose. Joey, at 17, joined the Army and headed off to Fort Ord

Joe in his parachute gear

for basic training, then to Fort Lewis in Washington for Advanced Infantry Training and finally to jump school to become a paratrooper.

Joe was so proud of his jump wings . I can still hear him humming, "I want to be an Airborne Ranger, lead a life of blood and danger. Airborne ... All the Way ... Airborne!"

While I was living in South San Francisco, Joe came home on leave just before he reported for duty in Vietnam. Vietnam? Where in hell is Vietnam? No one had really heard of it; we had to go to the library and look at a world atlas to find it. Seems like there was a little war going on there that no one thought would last long. I arranged a small going-away party with beer and music for him, just a few friends and a couple of my girlfriends. Joe was in the kitchen talking to his buddies and I overheard him say, "If I get zapped [the first time I heard that word ... he meant shot, badly wounded, crippled or maimed], I don't want to come home." "What?" I cried aloud. He didn't know I could hear him because I was in the living room. I began to cry. Joe came over to me and kneeled beside me and said, "Sis, don't worry, I'm coming home." I told him, "I've always looked after you, I'm supposed to look after you, but now I can't." Joe looked at me and said, "It's okay. I'll be home in a year, don't worry sis." He promised. I stopped crying because I believed him. Of course he would be coming home. After all, he was just going to some small place in the world called Vietnam. He left on August 31, 1967.

> **Where in hell is Vietnam? No one had really heard of it; we had to go to the library and look at a world atlas to find it.**

Shortly after Joe's party, Al and I moved again, this time to Millbrae, California, where my son Craig started first grade and Destiny started kindergarten. We soon moved from Millbrae, because Al nearly set our duplex on fire when he fell asleep while smoking and dropped his cigarette on the sofa. Of course, he was drunk (patterns, anyone?). Thank God I woke up in the middle of the night, choking on smoke. While Al crawled on the floor, dragging the sofa out the front door,

I pulled the kids out of bed and took them out the back door to the yard. After the firemen put out the fire, the landlord politely asked us to move. So we moved (again) to San Carlos, a neighboring town of San Mateo, where we rented a small, but cute, corner house with a nice backyard. No more cold, wet weather in South San Francisco. The Bay Area, where we were headed, was warm and full of sunshine. Best of all, my grandmother moved in with us to help take care of the kids and help us with the rent. It was wonderful to have her in my daily life again. Oh, and the wonderful smells from the kitchen!

A World Gone Mad

I got a great job in San Mateo, working for First California Loans. It was a small one-girl office, a job they called a "Girl Friday." I did everything in the office: typed loans, answered phones, filed paper-work, etc. What was so special about my job was my boss, Ron Wright, who was truly a great guy. In between mortgages when business was slow, Ron — who read three or four newspapers each day and also was a bit of a history buff — would sit in my office and we would get into deep discussions on just about every subject. We talked a lot about politics, or rather, at the ripe old age of 25, I listened while Ron spoke of world events, particularly the Vietnam War. Because Joe was going there, I became interested in the war. The year was 1967/68, and it was if the world had gone mad. Thinking back now, it seemed as if nothing but bad things were happening in this timeframe: the Robert Kennedy and Martin Luther King, Jr., assassinations, the riots at the Chicago Democratic Convention, the flag and draft-card burnings, the protestors, the draft dodgers, and later the tragedy at Kent State. The more I learned, the less I felt in control of life and what was happening. This would be the seed that would grow and later lead me to act.

> The more I learned, the less I felt in control
> of life and what was happening.

To Dream the Impossible Dream

I regret that I didn't write Joe as often as I could or should have.
Mom would write him almost daily and when she received a letter
from him, she would call and read it to me. I remember his first
letter to me. He was so proud of the unit he was assigned to! He was
a paratrooper with the legendary 101st Airborne Division, known
universally as "the Screaming Eagles." Joe was an infantry paratrooper, and make no mistake, not just a Soldier but a "paratrooper."
He was so happy that he had gotten his jump wings so that he could
serve with the best. He was excited and spoke of maybe joining the
Green Berets someday. As I had mentioned, my boss Ron Wright
was a history buff. He told me of the famed Screaming Eagles history
during WWII. He explained how the 101st parachuted behind the
beaches ahead of the landings on D-Day and were surrounded by
the Germans during the Battle of the Bulge and prevailed. "*Wow,*"
I thought. "*My kid brother is serving with that Division — how cool
was that!*" I wrote back to my brother and told him how proud I was
of him. At 19, he was already a sergeant leading his 12-man squad
in combat. As months went by, Joe's letters changed, and as I began
to praise him, he replied, "Sis, you don't know what's going on over
here. I'm not what you think I am ..." I didn't understand that letter
or why he said that. Then Mom called me with a poem she had
received from him. I don't believe he wrote it but he sent it to her:
author unknown.

ODE TO A SOLDIER'S MOTHER

A Soldier's mother worries
When he goes to war.

She wonders if he is safe and happy,
Or if she will see him anymore.
She knows he doesn't want this war,
But she can also realize
He is fighting for a freedom,
This freedom is their lives.
I don't want this war.
But people, hear my voice;
I am fighting for something special,
My mother's right of choice.
So if I should die in combat,
Mother please don't weep;
For I would rather die protecting you
Than die while I'm asleep.
If God should take me unto Him,
During hate, hostility and war,
Remember Mother, I love my country,
But I love you even more …

Meanwhile, news of the war in Vietnam was televised daily and we watched the battles in our living rooms and at our dinner tables. I thought nothing could happen to Joe — after all, he was with the best Soldiers in the world and had told me over and over that he would be home in a year. He always ended his letters, "See you in September." "See You in September" was a popular song by The Happenings in 1966.[5] I can't believe that, after all these years, I can remember the words:

"I'll be alone each and every night, while you're away, don't forget
to write. Bye-bye, so long, farewell. Bye-bye, so long. See you in
September. See you when the summer's through."

> He was with the best Soldiers in the world and had told me over and over that he would be home in a year. He always ended his letters, "See you in September."

I think the reason I'm being so honest and open with my personal life in the initial chapters of this book is because of how I was affected by my trip to Vietnam in 1968, which you will read about in later chapters. As I stood on those mountain-top landing zones (LZs) talking to the young boys of the 327th Infantry, I was horrified to see that those boys, five to seven years my junior, looked like old men. Gaunt, prematurely wrinkled faces with eyes that looked past me in a haunted stare, and the crooked smiles. Battle had

Steve showing the effects of six months in continuous combat

stripped them down to their bare humanity. They had, as others in Vietnam would later recount, "lived in unrelenting stress and endured unimaginable horrors ... carrying everything they needed on their backs; constant vigilance around the clock; unending danger; spirit-draining, back-breaking, and exhausting labor; and an existence almost devoid of such creature comforts as frequent baths, clean clothes, beds, and uninterrupted nights."* I didn't know it then, but later life's lessons would teach me that I needed to tell their story as honestly as I could.

---

* Chaplain Claude Newby, *It Took Heroes: A Cavalry Chaplain's Memoir of Vietnam*, Presidio Press, 2003.

Now that I'm confessing all, I will tell you that after maturing,
I realized that my mission in life was to communicate the promise
I made to my brother and to honor him at every turn. I never
thought that my younger brother would be the one to change my
life's direction with his death, or that the pain and agony thrown at
me would change *me* beyond belief.

> **I realized that my mission in life was to communicate the promise I made to my brother and to honor him at every turn.**

My path has been a winding one, sometimes including ill-advised
decisions, uncharted paths, course corrections and big discoveries.
Ultimately, though, I ended up where I am supposed to be, sharing
a message of understanding and doing my very best to provide unity
where it is most needed.

Chapter 3
As High as the Clouds

Then came the letter from Joe that changed my life.

It was Christmas 1967 and he wrote, "Sis can you do me a favor ...? The morale in my company is low and dropping daily." I read between his lines: most of the guys didn't receive any mail, and in some cases they received hate mail. The news coverage of the war from back home seemed to filter through those horrid jungles and rice patties onto the battlefield, telling our boys fighting and dying about protest marchers telling young men to flee to Canada, to burn their draft cards and to turn our flag upside down in protest of the war. Fear and dissent about the war translated to a sense that Americans didn't support the Soldiers who were fighting that war. Joe let us know they had been in heavy contact with the enemy for months now, taking huge casualties and, "at home, they are calling us 'baby killers.' Doesn't anyone know that we are fighting for what we believe is necessary to keep freedom, and solely for the purpose of setting others free. Hasn't anyone reported the battles we've won against a battle-hardened, tough enemy — the NVA (North Vietnamese Army)?"

"Sis, What would be great is if the people at home started writing to us, and maybe even send us a few things from home just so we knew that the people back home cared. I know that this is a long-shot, but

I remember visiting your office just days before I was scheduled to leave for Vietnam, and what a nice town San Mateo was, and that people greeted me with a smile when I was in this uniform, so ... maybe you could get the City of San Mateo to adopt us. It would bring our morale up as high as the clouds, please try Sis."

So I did.

He's Not from Vietnam ...

I took Joe's letter to work and showed my boss, Ron Wright, and asked him to help me. Ron began to immediately help me compose a letter to city officials. He suggested that we try San Francisco first because that's where my brother and I were from. So we sent a letter to the U.S. Congressman and Mayor Alioto. The reply was that they were sorry but San Francisco had already adopted an aircraft carrier. So Ron and I figured, "OK, let's try San Mateo." It took three months to get a response and notification that it was on the city leadership's agenda for discussion for March 4, 1968.

I remember the excitement of going to my first City Council meeting and wondering if it mattered that Joe was not from San Mateo and that my only connection to the city was that I worked there. When the City Council came to the business of discussing Joe's request, that a young Soldier's unit be adopted by the City, Ron and I listened closely. Council members began to openly discuss Joe's request. "Was this young man from San Mateo? No." There was an uncomfortable silence. Hearing nothing but silence and seeing the negative looks on the faces of Council members, in desperation and before a vote of no could be put forward, I rose to my feet and said, "My brother is not from Vietnam either, but he is fighting their war."

After my unsolicited outburst, I meekly sat down. The Mayor stared at me for the longest time. I was trembling, partly in frustration but also in fear. I was thinking, *"Oh you've done it this time, Linda, you spoke before you thought."* Then the Mayor addressed the City Council members. All he said was, "This unit is part of the 101st Airborne Division ... anyone should be proud to adopt these para-troopers." With that simple state-ment, it was done. The Council passed a resolution adopting

Joe during a bout with malaria

Joe's unit, Alpha Company, 1st Battalion, 327th Airborne Infantry, 1st Brigade, 101st Airborne Division. I was appointed by the Council to lead the support in the community. I had no clue what I had gotten myself into, but I was eager to take on the challenge.

> ## I had no clue what I had gotten myself into, but I was eager to take on the challenge.

Vera Graham, a reporter who covered issues related to Council meet-ings, telephoned me and asked for a photo of Joe and an interview with me. The story of Joe's request and City Hall's approval of it ran as a cover story in *The San Mateo Times* on March 4, 1968. God, I was so excited! The only minor problem I could see was that I didn't really know where to start, except to immediately send Joe the front-page story about his unit being adopted by San Mateo, California.

Vera Graham gave me a list of leaders in the community — influential, well-connected people who might help me rally support. One of these individuals was San Mateo's Fire Chief, Noe Chanteloup. I made an appointment to meet the Chief. He was so wonderful and helpful. He gave me names of bank leaders, schools, and his own civic club, the Lions Club, who might help me. On March 15th, Joe wrote thanking me and the City Council and enclosed a handwritten roster of paratroopers' names. Finally, I could begin to get names out to people who were willing to write letters and send the troops "care packages." That was a start. It was a good start.

Chapter 4

Rainy Days and Mondays Always Get Me Down[6]

March 25, 1968

It was Monday, as if that wasn't bad enough. There was a rainy, cold chill-you-to-the-bone drizzle that had settled over the San Francisco area and the weather report said it wasn't going to improve anytime soon. Earlier in the day, I had been telephoned by a ladies' organization in Burlingame (a neighboring community on the north end of San Mateo) and was asked if I could drop by to see the first of the care packages they were about to send out to Joe and his buddies. I left work a bit early and raced over as fast as the law and traffic conditions would allow. I was met at the front door by Mrs. Thelma Castle, a sweet older woman who led me to the room were the packages were being prepared. Oh my! What a beautiful sight! All the packages were full of goodies that the Soldiers would love. Mrs. Castle pulled out a package that had been boxed especially for Joe and asked if I wanted to slip in a special note for him. Of course I did.

I individually thanked each woman and told her that they were doing God's work.

On the drive home, the sloppy weather and bumper-to-bumper traffic didn't seem to bother me. All I thought about was how wonderful it was for those women to donate their time for such a worthy cause. I imagined the goofy, silly grin that Joe would have on his face when he and his buddies received their care packages. I didn't even mind that I caught myself humming "See You in September" again.

When I pulled my car into the driveway at home, I thought it was strange to see Al, my husband, standing outside in the drizzle without a raincoat or umbrella, and with a serious expression on his face. As soon as Al walked up to the car, the drizzle changed to a hard rain that pelted his face. I rolled the window down and Al said in a barely audible tone, "Linda, Joe's been killed."

"What? What did you say?"

He repeated himself. That can't be right. Did I hear him right? It just can't be. I had just come from a group of ladies who were sending packages to him and his buddies. I had written him a little note to go in the box.

"No Al, you're wrong."

"Linda, I'm not. I wished to God that I was. Your mom called an hour ago with the news."

I backed out of the driveway without bothering to look; I was in a confused, dazed state of mind. I had to see my mom. I drove as fast as I could to her house, breaking all posted speed limits and warning signs. How I operated a car in such a stupor, I'm not sure. This was a mistake ... the U.S. Army had made a terrible mistake and I must tell her. Finally arriving, I ran from my car across my mom's rain-soaked lawn. I don't remember if I shut the car door or even bothered to turn the ignition off.

I burst through her front door and found Mom crying hysterically, "Linda, Joe is dead, they're sending him home."

Ed, my youngest brother, had a bloody fist from punching a wall. He hadn't wanted to believe it when the Army sedan drove up to the front of the house. He hadn't wanted to accept it when they told my mother, her husband Vic, and him that Joe had been killed in action.

I didn't want to allow it to be true. I told Mom that the Army is always making mistakes. I'd read about it often. I'm almost positive it's a mistake. It couldn't be true. "It's not Joe, Mom!"

"No!" Mom cried out, "It's been confirmed that Joe was killed in action yesterday, Sunday, March 24th."

And He Will Raise You Up on Eagles' Wings[7]

The days leading up to Joe's funeral were a blur. I don't remember driving home from my mother's or if I even did drive myself home that rainy Monday night after I had heard the dreadful news. I only remember being in bed for days, with the covers pulled over my head. I hadn't even changed out of my street clothes before I crawled into bed. I just lay in bed, not even responding to anyone who checked on me. Different organizations called to talk about care packages for the troops. I acknowledged none of them. I wanted it all to go away. What was the point of anything? Joe was gone.

The Army finally returned Joe's body to us. Again, I don't know if it took them days or weeks to do so. Joe's funeral and interment was held at Golden Gate National Cemetery. In the moment, nothing fully

ON THE VIETNAM MEMORIAL WALL

Panel 46E, Line 2
Joseph Gregory Artavia

PERSONAL DATA:

Home of Record:	San Francisco, CA
Date of birth:	01/01/1949

MILITARY DATA:

Service:	Army of the United States
Grade at loss:	E5
Rank/Rate:	Sergeant
ID No:	18905412
MOS/RATING:	11B4P: Infantryman (Airborne Qual)
Length Service:	01
Unit:	A CO, 1ST BN, 327TH INFANTRY, 101ST ABN DIV, USARV

CASUALTY DATA:

Start Tour:	08/31/1967
Incident Date:	03/24/1968
Casualty Date:	03/24/1968
Age at Loss:	19
Location:	Thua Thien Province, South Vietnam
Remains:	Body recovered
Casualty Type:	Hostile, died outright
Casualty Reason:	Ground casualty
Casualty Detail:	Gun or small arms fire

URL: www.VirtualWall.org/da/ArtaviaJG01a.htm

registered, like whether the day was sunny and bright or cloudy and cold. I remember stepping out of a car dressed in black from head to toe. I don't remember dressing; perhaps a family member dressed me. On each side of me were two people supporting my body weight, guiding me along the walkway to the chapel. Standing alongside the path that led to the pavilion where Joe lay in state were Mayor John Murray and other city officials of San Mateo, as well as hundreds of strangers. As we approached, I saw for the first time Joe's casket draped with an American flag. I could go no further ... I broke from my escorts and embraced one of the marble columns that supported the pavilion. The feel of the marble on my flesh was as cold as death. The funeral mass was performed, the eulogy was delivered, and a newspaper article was read aloud: SAN MATEO'S NUMBER ONE SON KILLED IN ACTION. I clung to that column until it was time to go.

Joe was posthumously awarded a Silver Star and Purple Heart. He was given full military honors, a 21-gun salute and, finally, the heart-wrenching notes of Taps were played by a lone bugler. Each. Note. Sounding. Shattering my heart.

Joe had promised to come home in September of '68. Instead, he left us March 24, 1968, forever. Our last hugs, kisses and goodbyes were in August '67. Joe's wishes were that his dad see him off. I think that was because his dad had served in WWII and knew what he would be facing. We didn't ...

A tribute to Joe

Chapter 5
Strength Through Sorrow

Joe's headstone at Golden Gate National Cemetery

"When we lose someone we love, it seems that time stands still.

What moves through us is a silence ... a quiet sadness ... a longing for one more day ... one more word ... one more touch.

We may not understand why you left this earth so soon, or why you left before we were ready to say good-bye, but little by little ... we begin to remember, not just that you died, but that you lived. And that your life gave us memories too beautiful to forget.

We will meet again someday, in a heavenly place where there is no parting.

A place where there are no words that mean good-bye."

— Bryan Smothers

Grieving

Fog. I was totally enveloped in a fog of my selfish grief. Not caring about the grief that my family members were experiencing, only my own, I wallowed in it. I never even thought of what pain Joe might have been in before he took his last breath. I thought of only the pain I was in. I was lost. My world had ended. Only later, much later, would I start to remember flashes of Joe's funeral. The one memory that haunts me to this day was the expression on my mother's face. It was that of a wounded animal, as if the bullet that ended Joe's life had pierced her heart as well.

> ## It was as if the bullet that ended Joe's life had pierced her heart as well.

"You left and I cried tears of blood. My sorrow grows. It's not just that you left. But when you left my eyes went with you. Now, how will I cry?"

— Rumi

On a Mission

A few days after Joe's funeral, the phone rang, and I reluctantly answered it. It was Vera Graham from *The San Mateo Times* inviting me to her office for a visit and to return Joe's photo, which she had borrowed for her stories. Somehow, I managed to shower, dress and find my way downtown to her office. After she poured me a cup of coffee, we sat in the lunchroom by ourselves. She opened a file and pulled out Joe's photo. After looking at it, she handed it to me. I ran my fingers across Joe's face. When I raised my face up, Vera, seeing the longing and sadness in my eyes, said, "Linda, think of Joe's last request to you. Think of what he wanted you to do. His buddies need you to carry on with this mission he gave you. It will keep his memory alive."

She was right ... a piece of my heart belonged to these men. Though the sorrow didn't stop, and he was not where I could see and touch him, I could still imagine his smile and hear his whisper. I could hear him saying, "This is good, sis ... stay on the trail, for our guys ... the brothers I've brought to you ..."

That was the turning point of my sorrow and mourning. I had to lock away the pain to accomplish what Joe wanted me to do. With her words in my head, I realized that I couldn't take care of my younger brother anymore, but I *could* take care of the 130 troopers I had adopted in Joe's place. I knew Joe's spirit would point me in the right direction and guide me through the mission he had tasked me with before his death. Joe would not be dead; he would live once again through the mission.

Vera Graham, by virtue of her position at *The San Mateo Times*, knew of people who could help me. Her contacts were invaluable. The first person I re-contacted was a wonderful man, Noe Chanteloup, San Mateo's Fire Chief, who was instrumental in helping with the first care packages. He was a sweet-looking little Frenchman with a heart bigger than I could imagine. He helped rally Lions Club members to write letters and to collect and send packages to the unit. He also welcomed any of our troopers who rotated home during the war, providing them accommodations with the firemen during their visit.

While Noe was the first to join me, many others followed. A wonderful woman called me after reading about Joe in the paper.

Her name was Barbara Schroeder. Barbara was a beautiful woman who lived in Hillsborough with her husband Hal and their children. She wanted to do something, so I asked her if she would become my co-chairman and help me go out in the community to rally support for San Mateo's adopted sons. While Barbara got her ladies' garden club involved, I went out to schools, spoke to the kids about our troopers

24—San Mateo *The Times* ★★★   Wed., Oct. 21, 1970

RESPONDING to the appeal to send holiday messages of cheer and remembrance to San Mateo's Adopted Sons in Vietnam are students of St. Gregory's Parochial School sixth grade. They are: Jim Kane, John Moore, Jim McCormick, Liane Conway, Gary McEntee and Patty Restaina. Letters, Christmas cards, gift packages are most urgently needed, say Co-chairmen Linda Giese and Barbara Schroeder. The adopted sons are members of "A" Co. 1-327 Inf. 1st Bn., 161st Airborne Div., APO 96383. San Francisco.   (Times Photo)

Students from St. Gregory's Parochial School mailing letters to the troops. Note: the future Mayor of San Mateo Maureen Freschet was Student President in the 8th grade at St. Gregory's and led the support campaign for her school.

and explained what a difference their letters would make to those fighting in faraway jungles. Noe had me speak to the Lions Club and from there I began to speak before any group who would listen — Rotary Clubs, The Elks, women's groups, American Legion Posts — asking all for their support.

In the local paper, Vera would print every trooper's letter that we provided to her. Our adopted sons of San Mateo wrote to us the feelings and thoughts they could not even reveal to their families. From day one, they were opening up to us about what they were facing on a day-to-day basis. They shared with us what it felt like to lose a friend in a firefight. And repeatedly, and importantly, they told us that they thought San Mateo was the only city in America that cared about them. They told us about how they couldn't wait to come home and meet some of the folks who were writing to them. I remember with every letter received, Barbara and I would immediately call one another reading our letter over the phone, so excited to hear from another one of our Soldiers.

As group leader, I would receive the Rosters from "A" Company. In the beginning, they called themselves "Assassins," then referred to themselves as "ABU," a name that derived from a photo of a monster holding a dagger in one hand, and pistol in the other hand. Apparently, as the story goes, one paratrooper had a nightmare of this monster and it would become the mascot of the unit, with the troopers calling it ABU! It was because of the Rosters that I could give out names and keep track of the troopers who needed a letter. To everyone I met or to whom I spoke, I offered a name. Calls would come into my office (I was still working for First California Loans) asking for the name of another trooper because, as many would say, "My trooper is home now and I need another name." This made it so worthwhile, knowing these young men had truly become our adopted sons.

Every Waking Hour

Barbara and I (and other volunteers) attended several events — like the San Mateo County Fair —to expose the public to San Mateo's Adopted Sons. We set up a booth and set up a male manne-quin in full paratrooper gear, which I was able to obtain on loan from the Presidio Army installation. We took shifts working our Screaming Eagle booth at the Fair, passing out names and telling of our City's adoption story. So many people took names and, even though they were probably against the war itself, they understood it was our Soldiers we supported.

I only recall one negative incident. Once when I returned from my lunch break at work (which was the only time I could break away to meet a new club, school or business, hoping to enroll their support), my boss Ron Wright mentioned that he got a call from the Rotary Club. They explained that they refused to hear me because they thought I was a War Monger. "Gee, what is that?" I asked, hearing the expression for the first time. Ron explained, and I felt saddened that they would think that of me. But I quickly shrugged it off, knowing there were others who cared. Happily, the local Rotary Club later changed their stance and voted to support us.

Imagining ways to support A Company consumed my every thought.

Imagining ways to support A Company consumed my every thought. When it was Halloween, my mind fired off, "God, wouldn't our troops just love candy!" So, with Linda Takenouchi, a good friend and confi- dante with whom I had grown up, I rented a car and a bull horn and drove up and down San Mateo and Hillsborough residential neighbor- hoods, asking to "Trick

Milo D'Anjou at the First Federal Savings Association with Brownie Troop 1202

or Treat" for our San Mateo Adopted Sons. I asked them to bring their candy to City Hall. It worked! We got a great deal of candy and quickly shipped it out to A Company. What fun that was! We both still laugh today thinking about it.

My children were also involved in our efforts. Craig and Destiny attended Laurel Elementary School in San Carlos, where they asked their classmates to write letters. I was so proud to see them handing the Principal all their class letters to be mailed to our troops. Vera insured that news articles were printed on a regular and constant basis. This regular exposure in the press helped guarantee that more community citizens, as well as people in the surrounding communities, became involved. One huge supporter was the

Children Write 160 Soldiers in Vietnam

Linda's children, Craig and Destiny, delivering letters for the soldiers to the San Carlos Postmaster H.J. (Bud) Johnson.

Burlingame Women's Club, located in a neighboring town of San Mateo. Thelma Castle of the Burlingame Club — who was the woman I spent that fateful morning with before finding out that Joe had been killed — approached the Golden Gate Federation of Women's Club for their involvement too. And, wow, with their support, it took off. Our Soldiers were getting wonderful care packages and letters from them as a result of Thelma's and the Clubs' support.

Thelma personally remembered World War II and the Country's overwhelming support for our servicemen and women. It was only fitting that these troops get the same attention. She felt strongly about supporting our Screaming Eagles, San Mateo's adopted sons. She worked feverishly through her Burlingame Women's Club.

Letters from Vietnam: Thank-You Notes Provide Food for Thought

A bit of food, some canned meat, foot powder, and candy were just a few of the items packaged by the members of the North Burlingame Women's Club and sent to the men of the 101st Airborne Division in Vietnam in memory of Joe Artavia. These packages were beginning to pay dividends in the form of thank you notes, some penned by flashlight, by the troopers after a day of war. These provided the club-women with some poignant food for thought.

Here are a few samples: Some are brief, some are long, but all speak volumes.

SGT Everett W. Kadle:

"Wish to express our deepest gratitude. The food was delicious, the books excellent. Such things are highly prized by us troopers. SGT Artavia was a fine NCO. Unfortunately, war seems to always choose our best men as its victims. Truly war is hell ... that about concludes this note, I guess ..."

SGT Dave Blosser:

"I am at this moment, back at our Base Camp, just a few miles south of Huế, writing this letter by flashlight, using a box as a desk. I am inside of my hooch, listening to some tape-recorded music sent from home, and I occasionally look over at my machine gun, hoping to get some inspiration, in writing this letter. Well, nothing comes to mind, so I'll just say what's in my mind. THANK YOU, thank you so much for the package you sent to me. It is the nicest thing to come my way in a long time of misery, eight months of it in this hell, known as Vietnam. I say this from my heart and I truly appreciate what you've done, and the time you've spent for us.

Steve with his men in Vietnam

Your note said in memory of Sergeant Artavia, I knew him well, and was in the fire fight that he was killed in, when he did a job that he knew to be dangerous and wouldn't let any of his men do it, to crawl forward, and out where the enemy was, and direct my machine guns to fire in support of the platoon. I know the risk he took, since he told me to stay with my guns (I have two in my squad — I'm the platoon support squad, or weapons squad) and to keep them both firing. He took my place, out there. One of my gunners was killed a few minutes before him, and I had to operate that gun, as well as control my other gun. Also, one of my other men, an ammo bearer, was wounded, shot in the face. No, I'll never forget Joe Artavia. We were buddies. And he gave his life for me, and the platoon. Again, I say thank you again for your confidence, and trust in us in Vietnam. You are the people, who are the important ones."

Specialist Fourth Class Carl A. Hillis, Jr:

"Thank you, and I want you to know that it's thoughtful people like you that make paratroopers like us realize that we must continue to fight even after we lose our close buddies on the battlefield."

And there are those who wrote more than once.

Specialist Fourth Class Vince Pikutis:

"SGT Artavia was in my platoon, we were friends, I was there when SGT Artavia died when my company attacked an enemy base camp. My company was fighting for two hours, then it ended. The sound of gun fire was silenced, and we went out to retrieve our fallen buddies. My platoon was very sad when Artavia's body was carried past our platoon. Most of us cried. He was a great guy. I don't know why God chose him so early in life."

Another time, he wrote: "You asked me about for my views. I think I'm too young (19) to understand this mixed up world. Sometimes I think I may never understand the actions of this country even when I am old and grey."

Chapter 6

Changes in Latitude, Changes in Attitude

The holidays were approaching, and for Thanksgiving I drove to Palo Alto, just a few miles south of San Mateo. There was a nightclub with a band. I thought it would be fun to ask the band if they would please dedicate their next number to our Screaming Eagles … and they did. They sang "Come Fly with Me."[8]I told them that the Screaming Eagles were Airborne Paratroopers, so I guess they thought they were pilots, but it didn't matter. What mattered was that the song was dedicated to our famed Screaming Eagles, I got it on my trusty tape recorder and that is all I wanted to hear.

Then the thought came, *"Why not have medallions made up for our Soldiers for Christmas?"* A special keepsake for them from us! The medallions would be nickel plated (to look like silver), with the City Seal, but instead of "Incorporated," it would say "Adopted Son." Using our Roster list, we would engrave each medallion with a Soldier's name on the back, with the date of the adoption 3-4-68. Then we could send these to our adopted sons in a Christmas card.

Do You Know the Way to … Vietnam?[9]

Al came up with the idea that I should personally visit ABU for Christmas. Now to work out the minor details! When I presented the plan to the City of San Mateo, they thought it was great. I would be their Ambassador. Mayor Archibald wrote an introduction letter for me, in the event that I needed it once entering Vietnam. My mission was to present our Christmas gift to A Company (ABU/Assassins) 1st Battalion, 327th Infantry, 1st Brigade, 101st Airborne Division — our Screaming Eagles.

Press photo of Linda on the night before her trip to Vietnam, 1968

Now how would I pay for the 16-hour flight to Vietnam? Al made calls and found a sorority, Pi Epsilon, who might help. The president of the sorority thought *"what a wonderful cause this would be"* and she came up with a $500.00 donation from their members toward the $1,000.00 it would cost to purchase a round-trip ticket to Vietnam on a civilian airline. We took a loan out for the additional $500.00 and purchased the ticket. Now all I needed was a passport and that was soon accomplished!

The evening of December 16, 1968, I stood before San Mateo's Mayor and Council members, preparing to leave for Vietnam. My flight was at 9:00 p.m., departing from San Francisco Airport via Pan American Airlines scheduled to arrive in Saigon the following day. I had sent a telegram to the Executive Officer, LT Stephen Patterson, to advise him of the details of my arrival, and figured my telegram would give him all the information he needed. It turns out, while he knew about my planned trip, he knew nothing about the details because he was back out in the field with his men at the time. LT Patterson and I had been corresponding to keep me updated on the troops and to provide me with the roster of those active, wounded and killed in action. This was very difficult, but something we had to expect. Sadly, the roster was in constant flux and there were many names with lines through them, indicating that they were either killed or wounded in action. Casualties were something I would need to tell people about and to be prepared if a letter, card or package was returned.

Article from *Pacific Stars and Stripes*,
December 17, 1968

I'll Be Home for Christmas[10]

The evening of my departure, as I stood before the Council and the Mayor, I felt excited and ready. The City of San Mateo provided a police escort for me to the San Francisco airport, but I had forgotten all my medallions! *Oh my God, they were in a suitcase, but still at my house!* We had to make a detour to pick them up before going to the airport. I guess with all the excitement of traveling, I had forgotten the reason for my trip. Oh well, blame it on my distracted state of mind. In any event, thanks to the San Mateo Police Department private escort, I made my flight in plenty of time.

DEPARTMENT OF THE ARMY
COMPANY A, 1ST BATTALION (AIRBORNE) 327TH INFANTRY
APO San Francisco 96347

COMPANY ROSTER

NAME	ASN	DOR	DEROS	ETS	PMOS	REMARKS
CPT						
JOHNSON, JULIUS F	~~OA180131~~	1NOV66	25JUL68	INDEF	71542	
1LT						
BISHOP, WILLIAM E	~~OA107598~~	8JUN67	12JUN68	INDEF	71542	
CARHART, THOMAS M III	~~OA107919~~	8JUN67	13DEC68	INDEF	71542	*Hosp*
HERNANDEZ, TARSICIO	~~OA984249~~	16NOV67	19OCT68	16NOV68	71542	
SANDERS, EDWARD B	~~OA100606~~	29JUL67	25MAY68	INDEF	71542	
WILSON, HARVEY L	~~OA330966~~	12MAY67	20JUL68	INDEF	71542	
2LT						
Patterson, Stephen J Jr		*14JAN68*	*14JAN69*	*13JAN69*	*71542*	
SMITH, RALPH W	~~OA228405~~	11NOV66	11NOV68	11NOV68	71542	*Hosp*
E-8						
DAYOC, JOSEPH J JR	~~RA12560189~~	13MAR64	9MAR68	14JUL68	11G5P	
E-7						
McNEIL, DANIEL J	~~RA14756198~~	20AUG66	7JAN69	21OCT68	11C4P	
URBAN, CLARENCE W	~~RA16725648~~	1APR67	27JUL68	7FEB68	11B4P	
E-6						
BORKOWSKI, MARIO	~~RA16642871~~	1NOV67	25SEP68	8JAN69	11C4P	
DOYLE, WILLIAM R	~~RA17280165~~	1OCT67	16FEB68	10JUN70	11B4P	
HEREFORD, TERRY S	~~RA19859875~~	25DEC67	14JUN68	8SEP68	11B4P	
PATTERSON, JOHN H	~~RA17494127~~	1JAN68	4MAR68	29APR68	11B4P	*DEROS*
SANDERS, BILLIE R	~~RA14550122~~	1OCT67	27JUN68	21JUL70	11B4P	*R&R*
SMITH, DELMAR	~~RA16969544~~	8AUG67	21OCT68	14JUL68	11B4P	
SOWERS, ARTHUR E	~~RA16500248~~	14JUL61	2SEP68	4AUG69	11H4P	*Hosp*
Tyler, Michael T		*13 Sep 67*	*16 Jan 69*	*9 Aug 70*	*11B4P*	
WATSON, LEON	~~RA18973166~~	5OCT63	27SEP68	29APR72	11B4P	
WILLIAMS, CHESTER	~~RA14926222~~	1JAN68	21SEP68	18AUG68	11B4P	
E-5						
ARTAVIA, JOE G	~~RA18000012~~	1JAN68	2SEP68	28NOV69	11B4P	*KIA*
BAKER, JAMES D	~~RA20000043~~	1OCT67	25JUL68	21MAR69	11C4P	
BATEMAN, THOMAS G	~~RA16007006~~	1JAN68	4MAR68	7AUG69	11B4P	

Department of the Army, First Line Roster, Company A, 1st Battalion (Airborne), 327th Infantry

Waiting at the airport was my mother Gloria. I could see the sadness in her eyes and the fear for me leaving to a war-torn country that had taken her son only a few months earlier. "Linda," she asked, "Why are you doing this?"

Linda with her mother, Gloria, at the airport

"For Joe, Mom. I hope you understand."

Turning around one last time to say goodbye, I said, "Mom, don't worry. The 101st will take care of me. I'll see you in two weeks."

Chapter 7
Vietnam – Where Eagles Dare

Mile One of 7,829.

Millions of thoughts raced through my mind.

"Would the 101st get my telegram in time?"

"What if no one was there to meet me?"

"What would I do in Saigon?"

"How would I get to the 101st, who I knew were hundreds of miles north of Saigon, in what was known as Northern I Corp and near the city of Huế?"

It was Huế that was the site of a month-long battle during the Tet Offensive when the North Vietnamese enemy had taken the ancient Citadel City.

I would later learn that The Battle of Huế (also called the Siege of Huế) was one of the bloodiest and longest battles of the Vietnam War. Just one month before Joe's death, the South Vietnamese city was suddenly awash with Soldiers and intense fighting. Ten battalions of the People's Army of Vietnam (PAVN or NVA) and the Viet Cong (VC) had attacked the city, which was ultimately successfully defended by the Army of the Republic of Vietnam (ARVN), the U.S. Army and the U.S. Marine Corps (a total of 16 battalions).

Huế's highway was an important supply line for ARVN, U.S. and Allied Forces, and was a base for U.S. Navy supply boats. And while the city should have been well defended from such an attack, our guys were taken by surprise when the Viet Cong and PAVN launched the Tet Offensive. Thousands of enemy combatants were killed, as were thousands of civilians, and the losses and injuries for the Allied Forces, while significantly less than what was suffered by the enemy, were heartbreaking. News of this battle had made it back home, of course, and the very thought of house-to-house combat further ignited negative sentiment about the war. Support from home began to wane even more. But I never stopped believing in our servicemen. San Mateo never stopped supporting them. I was flying 7,829 miles to prove to them that we cared.

I was flying 7,829 miles to prove to them that we cared.

The flight from America was long. I thought of Joe and his buddies, and I began to feel excited that I was going to see them face to face. They were my brothers, my heroes! I had nothing to fear ... they would look after me and make sure nothing would happen. I had two very brief layovers, for maybe a half hour in Hawaii and Guam, then on to Vietnam a short four hours away. I couldn't wait. Not many people were on the plane — just a few Soldiers. One I sat near showed me a news article he was reading in the *San Francisco Examiner* — it was about me leaving for Vietnam to visit our Soldiers. Wow, our story made the San Francisco paper and even had a picture of me holding Joe's picture.

I slept little, if at all. I was too excited. As we were about to land, I thought, *"Joe you won't be here to see me, but I know you are here with me. Why Joe, why did you have to get killed? Remember what you told me? You promised you would come home. You were so young, Joe … only 19."*

"Why? Why?" I kept asking myself as I grew nearer to where he spent his last days fighting. For some reason I would be closer than I had ever been with Joe. As I looked down at the rice paddies from my window, I knew you were there, Joe.

In-Country

The big silver Pan Am bird spiraled carefully down and landed at Tan Son Nhat Airport, Vietnam. Vietnam! *Can you believe it, Vietnam!* As we taxied to the terminal, I looked out the window and prayed, *"Please dear God, let them be here for me, please …"* Then I saw a jeep and two Soldiers. The first thing I recognized was the Screaming Eagle Patch on their shoulders. One of the Soldiers had a Ranger Tab above his Eagle Patch. Oh My God, they sent an Army Ranger to pick me up. Thank you dear Lord, they are here!

I stepped off the plane and was almost knocked off my feet by a humidity-laden blast of furnace-hot wind that blew across the tarmac. I was wearing big dark Audrey Hepburn style sunglasses that immediately fogged, and my hair frizzed so much so that I resembled Sly of Sly and the Family Stone fame.[11] I started wilting, and what an odor that hung in the air. Strange … I had never smelled anything like it.

The Soldier wearing the Ranger Tab jumped from the jeep that had pulled up next to the plane and walked up to me. He was handsome, dark tanned and looked very Italian. And did I mention that he was handsome? The young lieutenant eyed me up and down, trying to peek behind my glasses, then asked "Are you Linda?" He later confessed that he thought for a moment that I was a Vietnamese woman behind those large sunglasses, but couldn't imagine them wearing a dress like I was wearing. Definitely American style (and zebra-print, no less!). "Yes," I said, and then he introduced himself: "I'm LT Patterson, Steve ... your military escort. The Company is looking forward to your visit ... everyone is excited!"

Linda's arrival in Vietnam, escorted from the tarmac by Steve (on right)

"Thank you, I'm excited to meet them too," I said. With that, he picked up my suitcases, threw them in the back of the jeep, helped me in and then we sped from the airfield. No one questioned us ... we just left. LT Patterson took me to Bien Hua, which was an In-Country training base for troops entering Vietnam. It was commanded by Colonel Harold Hayward, who greeted us (and that handshake became an iconic photo, included on the cover of this book). There, we would catch a military plane, a C-130, up to Camp Eagle (the 101st Northern rear base).

I was informed that they had made arrangements for me to sleep at the Nurses HHQ in Phu Bai, but that I would be spending all my time at Camp Eagle, and that A Company (ABU) — our adopted Company — was in the jungle but would be coming in as soon as they could to meet me. Steve was very attentive to me on the C-130 cargo plane on the flight up country. He pointed out the South China Sea and described the many bomb craters. He told me about the unit, explaining that it was a very special unit and their paratroopers were very special men. He went on to say that the 1st Brigade reported for combat duty in Vietnam in July of 1965. The Brigade operated sepa-rately from the Division, which was still garrisoned at Fort Campbell, Kentucky, until December 1967. During those two and a half years, the Brigade fought in 24 locations. Wherever there was a hotspot, General Westmoreland would send the Brigade.

Including the upcoming three-day stand down for Christmas, the men had only nine days of rest. So for 356 days of the year, they humped the mountains jungle, tracking down the enemy. They carried between 120 and 150 lbs. of equipment each and had no hot meals, only C Rations. Every night, they slept on the jungle floor and every day they were on the move. He doubted that any other unit operated the way the Brigade did and with the demands that were placed on the men. He thanked me for all the support coming from San Mateo, saying the Soldiers couldn't believe it. San Mateo was the only city from home that wrote them. He also told me what a tough time the unit had, how they had been engaged in heavy combat situations on an almost daily basis. Again, LT Patterson spoke of the men (boys, for the most part), who were incredible Soldiers, then he recounted the honor he felt serving and leading these men. I was just awestruck. We civilians had no idea of what these men endured.

He mentioned that I would be meeting Major General Zais, 101st Division Commander. While I listened to Steve, I thought of how lucky I was to be among such great Soldiers, great Americans, such courageous young men. I thought of Joe writing me, telling me he wished I could meet his brothers. And now, they were all my brothers, and, yes, San Mateo's "Adopted Sons."

Phu Bai

Top left: Tactical Operation Command (TOC) post on Fire Base Tomahawk; Top right: Cobra attack helicopter; Bottom: Linda's sleeping quarters at the MASH unit in Phu Bai

The flight to Phu Bai (pronounced "fu by") flew by ... sorry, bad pun. The C-130 cargo plane landed, well ... bounced ... down the runway. Not what I would call the smoothest of landings. We laughed then made a comment to the pilot that it was a little on the rough side for a civilian. LT Patterson took me to a bunk, sleeping quarters (hooch?) in the nurses and doctors area where I would be staying/sleeping, and told me he would be picking me up in an hour to take me over to Camp Eagle to meet some of the Soldiers in the rear. Also, General Zais would like me to be his guest at dinner that evening.

Steve then gave me three sets of fatigues to wear, saying it would probably be easier to get in and out of helicopters wearing jungle fatigues and boots. I couldn't believe he had my name and San Mateo sewn on the jacket, along with a Ranger Tab. I beamed with pride when I put that jacket on. When Joe initially went in, the 101st was made up of paratroopers only ... it was the history of the 101st. But later, this was no longer a requirement because of the attrition rate ... there were not enough paratroopers to replace them.

Next to my hooch sleeping quarters were signs that read: "Don't feed the rats." *God, Lieutenant, what is this all about?* He just smiled at my obvious dismay.

"On My Command ... Release Hell!"

During my first day at Camp Eagle, I just hung out and talked to everyone about home. Steve had worked out a busy itinerary for me; first on the agenda was a visit to Artillery Fire Base Tomahawk. To safely get to the Fire Base, we had to fly by helicopter, in a Huey, the work horse of Vietnam. They actually let me sit up front and take the controls. I know the pilot had control, but they had fun letting me think I was flying.

When we arrived at the fire base, and once the dust storm from the helicopter's rotor settled down, I smelled a distinctive odor that hung in the air, such a strange smell. I saw young paratroopers burning something in cut-down 55- gallon drums. I asked what they were burning but never got an answer, only a smile. So I'm guessing they were burning classified reports, ha ha!

There was a captain who greeted us and was grinning from ear to ear. He introduced himself as the BC (Battery Commander). He said, "Welcome to luxurious FB Tomahawk, the best kept secret in all of Vietnam and home to 'No Slack.'" The thought that ran through my mind was ... *luxurious?* It's a hill in the middle of nowhere. They joked a lot. The

"No Slack" Artillery Fire Base Tomahawk

curiosity of the Soldiers around me was beyond belief, like *"where did you come from?"* The captain began to explain what their job was, and the importance of the Fire Base location, then he walked us over to the area they called TOC (Tactical Operations Center). I descended some dirt steps into an underground bunker, which was such a confining area with large maps pinned on the wall. Pointing at a map, they started to explain to me where the enemy NVA was. I listened and tried to understand as they described a tactical assault. Of course, it went right over my head. When I climbed out of the bunker, I understood why Steve had fatigues tailored for me ... my mini skirt would really had been a problem.

Once back outside, we walked over to a 105mm howitzer, a piece of artillery that looked like a canon. They loaded it, gave me a set of binoculars and pointed at a hill in the distance and said that was going to be the point of impact. Before firing they said, "You want to kill a few enemy? All you have to do is pull the lanyard [a line/

Linda firing a 105mm howitzer with "No Slack" 2/320 FAR (Forward Artillery Regiment), 101st ABN (Airborne Division), December 1968

cord]. Here ... you will need these ear plugs." So I stuck the plugs in my ears, stood where I was told to and on the officer's command, I pulled the lanyard as hard as I could. WOW! The howitzer recoiled with a deafening roar, a dust cloud covered the area and cordite burned my eyes and nose. The guys laughed and congratulated me. The officer that was looking through a set of binoculars said, "Linda, look at that distant hill at about two-o'clock, wait for it ... wait for it." Then there was a flash, a puff of smoke and a faraway muted "whomp" sound. "Good shooting Linda. I think you may have just killed some of the enemy." For a minute, I thought to myself ... *paybacks are hell ... for you Joe, for you.*

During my short visit at the FSB, the guys pounded out from a brass shell a bracelet for me, and even engraved it "To Linda from A Batt." I thanked them and put it on my wrist. What a treasure!

We flew off to another Fire Base, and this one was to be a surprise for the men. Steve thought it would be nice if I served the men lunch as they walked through the line, and to their amazement ... there I was, putting food on their plates. Gosh, they were so young. Some smiled and others just had a look of *"Where did you come from, lady?"* After serving up lunch, I sat down with them on something that looked like a bench, and we began to talk. Small talk, like what's new in the World (as they referred to it), telling me where they were from, and that they definitely planned to stop by San Mateo when they rotated home. They all would eventually DEROS (Date Eligible for Return from Overseas), through Travis Air Base, Oakland, and then to San Francisco Airport. I told them we would pick them up, and they would definitely have a place to stay for however long they wanted to visit.

Our conversations were full of laughter and stories of home. I did a lot of posing for pictures. Slipping an arm around my waist or shoulder for a picture with them seemed awkward to some of those hardcore Soldiers, as if I would break. Back on the Huey, flying back to Camp Eagle, I thought about the day's events, the guys I met and how it seemed like a dream. I had the biggest smile on my face. Aside from having my children, coming to Vietnam was the most important thing I'd ever done.

FYI

ABU is pronounced A-BOO. The earliest mentions of the "Abu" seems to originate during the 1st Airborne Battle Group period of the early 1960s. Units started using animal names as unit call signs during this period. Units designated B, C and D companies had no problem coming up with animal nicknames (e.g., Bobcat, Cougars and Dogs), but "A" companies had a harder time. So A/1-327 came up with the Abu. It has been said that ABU means Air Borne Unit, and many grunts will tell you it means "A" company, Best Unit. Why? Because it is. Popular belief is that it was concocted from a nightmare that the company commander had. It had a gorilla body, a moose's head with antlers, an alligator tail, and was clutching a pistol in the right hand

and a knife with blood dripping in the left. If the antlers don't get you, then the gator tail will.

ABU six ... ABU six ... This Is Big Mama ...Over

The men hacking their way through the jungle wanted to hear from me, so I would speak to them over the radio. My call sign was "Big Mama" (at 27 years old, I hated that call sign), but I was informed that the Battalion Commander's call sign was "Big Daddy," so I guess it was okay. In my mind, I worried that my brothers would see me as a "Big Mama" and not a sister, the image I wanted them to have. After all, I *was*

In front of A Company orderly room, Camp Eagle

their sister! When I spoke to them over the radio, it was awkward and strange, but I felt like I knew them all my life and couldn't wait to see them in the flesh. I wanted them to know why I was there, not just for San Mateo, but for all of America as well. I wanted them to know how proud we were of each and every one of them, and that we cared and loved them with all our hearts and souls. They were our heroes. Contrary to what they heard, read about happenings at home, or the treatment many of their fellow Soldiers received upon returning home, the dissent or indifference wasn't what America really thought of them. Because *real* America was alive in towns like San Mateo, California ... we connected, we bonded, we cared.

> ### *Real* America was alive in towns like San Mateo, California ... we connected, we bonded, we cared.

One day, while waiting for ABU to stand down, one Soldier came up to LT Steve and asked if I could drive the Mule. The Mule was a mail cart, looked like fun, and I for sure wanted to give it a try. I almost drove it through the orderly room because I couldn't find the brakes — everyone had a good laugh with that. A heartwarming moment was when one of the Soldiers turned 18 (I'll repeat myself, just turned 18). We had a cake with candles and sang "happy birthday" to that young Soldier. For a moment — a very brief moment — it was like home for us and that young boy.

Every day that LT Patterson came to pick me up, he had to wait a few minutes. I was always a little late getting myself together. God it was really early, I don't know, maybe 7:00 a.m. One day, at the crack of dawn before the rooster crows, he picked me up to visit a grade school that was driving distance from the base. He introduced me to the Vietnamese children as "mama-san," a name for mother or a woman in authority. The class I visited

Linda visits with a Vietnamese village school, waiting for troops coming in from the jungle, December 1968 (in background is PIO SGT John Neely)

greeted me by singing "Oh My Darling, Clementine"[12] in English ... what a treat that was! The kids followed us everywhere ... I'm sure I was a strange-looking creature to them, an American woman walking among Soldiers. The children offered me sugar cane sticks, touched my fatigues jacket, my hands, made me think of my own kids back home and how much I missed them.

> **The children offered me sugar cane sticks, touched my fatigues jacket, my hands, made me think of my own kids back home and how much I missed them.**

Still waiting for ABU to come in, LT Patterson told me that he was taking me to Huế for the day. It was nearby so we would go by jeep; a machine gunner would accompany us. Steve wanted me to see the historical Citadel and where the Tet Offensive took place just earlier that year. When we arrived, I was amazed at seeing the wall and the ruins of that Huế Battle scenes. Then it seemed that, out of nowhere, three little Vietnamese kids showed up, asking if they could be our guides. Steve understood them referring over and over to me as Number 1 ... They took us into the Citadel, where there were beautiful shrines, temples and bejeweled Buddha figures on pedestals. It was incredible. As we walked through the Citadel and came out, LT Patterson noticed a lone Vietnamese man dressed in black pajamas and sandals, sitting on a bicycle, smiling at us. Steve felt uneasy, thinking that the guy staring at us looked like a Viet Cong (enemy). Without hesitation, he turned to me and told me to get back in the jeep. I noticed his hand griping his weapon and, without a word spoken and just with his eyes, the warning he gave his machine-gunner. To this day, Steve believes that Soldier was an enemy combatant and admits that, because of my presence, he made a quick decision to let the man ride off on his bicycle without incident.

At long last, ABU would be coming in the next day. I wanted to look my best for my brothers, but my hair had a mind of its own. It had been so frizzy because of the Vietnam monsoon weather that I couldn't manage it. Steve told me one of the Soldiers in the rear said he had a hair salon back in the

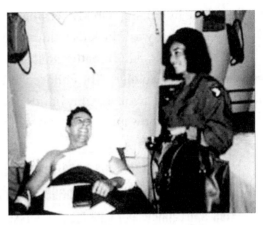

Linda brings cheer to the wounded

states and would be willing to set my hair. Great! I had wisely thought to bring hair rollers, and now I had my very own French coiffeur! This was going to be awesome. I walked over to the hooch, I mean my salon, and there he was holding a comb and brush, and a bunch of Soldiers just sitting around wanting to watch. "Okay," I said. "What can you do with my hair?" He began to brush through it over and over. I handed him a few rollers and said that they might help. The Soldier kept brushing my hair, looked at a roller I had handed him and seemed quite puzzled about what do I do with it. I looked at him, laughed and asked if he really had a hair salon back in the States. "No, it was my wife's." The solders watching roared with laughter! I handed my jungle fatigue cladded hairdresser a bobby pin and showed him where to put it in the roller. He was a good sport, and so was I. After all was said and done, my hair came out great and I was ready to face ABU.

Chapter 8

Peace on Earth, Good Will to Men[13]

At last, on the following morning, I could see the Chinook helicopters bringing in the men. ABU Is in the House!

> I must admit that while waiting to meet my "brothers," I was a ball of nerves.

While the Company assembled, Lieutenant Patterson hid me away in the company orderly room. I must admit that while waiting to meet my "brothers," I was a ball of nerves. I was on the verge of a paralyzing anxiety attack. I was short of breath, my pulse was racing and my heart was in my throat. To calm myself and to occupy my mind while the Company Commander, Captain Christian Shore, talked to his men, I studied the orderly room. It had a dirt floor, the walls were sandbags stacked eight-feet high, the roof was a combination of huge timbers, steel plating, and then more sandbags piled on top three-feet thick. There was a dark green file cabinet that had seen better days, three mismatched chairs and wooden ammo crates stacked up with a sheet of plywood on top to create a makeshift desk. In the center of the desk was an ancient typewriter, a stack of carbon typing paper, a coffee cup, a half dozen M-16s, hand grenades, several fully packed rucksacks that weighed over 100 pounds each, mosquito repellent, a copy of the *Stars and Stripes* newspaper, and a can of C Ration peaches.

The walls had a great poster of a combat Soldier, a poster of three officers and — to my surprise — a photo of me and San Mateo Mayor Roy Archibald. The orderly room had a few Christmas decorations as a reminder it was, after all, Christmas. I could hear everything happening on the other side of the wall and when Captain Shore started talking about me, I closed my eyes and conjured up a mental image of Joe, then my eyes filled with tears. My mind was filled with images of my little brother. I was in my own little world when Lieutenant Patterson touched my shoulder, startling me. He said "Linda, it's time. It's time to meet the men."

I slowly walked outside and the Captain introduced me, "This is Linda Giese, Joe's sister, and she has flown all the way from San Mateo, California, to spend Christmas with us." There was a little over 100 of them and they had just come out after four months straight in the mountainous jungle.

ABU upon returning from the jungle

I subconsciously looked for Joe's face among them, knowing he wasn't physically there, but I knew he was in spirit.

Not having had time to clean up, they wore tattered, muddy, sweat-stained and rain-soaked jungle fatigues they had worn for months. Their faces were gaunt and hollow, scratched and dirty, and ... oh my ... they were so young. I was somehow expecting older men, like in the movies, but standing before me at parade rest were young boys/men. They stared back at me ... then they smiled ... and my heart just melted. I began to speak to them, but what I really wanted to do was to run up to each one of them, hug them, give them all a sisterly kiss on the cheek and say, "We love you, we care about you." But instead I began telling them that I was there because of one special city in America. San Mateo. I told them how much we loved them, cared about them, and how very, very proud we were of them. Then I told them about the small Christmas gift we wanted them to have, a token from the people back home. The people of San Mateo, young and old, had sent me to present a small token of our appreciation on behalf of the Mayor, City Council, and all the citizens of San Mateo. It was small in size, only the size of a nickel, but what it carried was the love and pride of the people at home. It was cast with the city seal and read "Adopted Son." Each medallion had one of their names inscribed on the back. We had placed each coin in an envelope with a Christmas card that read:

"May the road rise up to meet you, may the wind be always at your back, may the sun shine warm upon your face, the rains fall soft upon your fields, and until we meet again, may God hold you in the palm of His hand."

I read the proclamation from the Mayor, and then began to call out their names. One by one, they shyly stepped forward, reached out for their Adopted Son medallion and thanked me. We had engraved the coins from the last company roster we had been furnished and,

Linda hands out the Christmas gifts from San Mateo

sadly, there were KIAs we had engraved coins for, and I didn't have coins for the new replacements. I felt terrible for them; what I should have done was bring some without names. I apologized to those without and promised we would send them. I think what was more important to them was that I was there representing a city from America that cared, and that may have been enough.

Once their commanding officers ordered them at ease, and they circled me and asked if I wouldn't mind taking a picture with them and their buddies. I was thrilled to stand alongside them with their arms around my waist or over my shoulder. The very shy ones were hesitant to speak with me, but finally came up and asked me a ton of questions. They asked about San Mateo, a city none of them knew of, but a city that cared so much about them. I asked where they were from — Georgia, Florida, Virginia, Texas — but, aside from their own immediate families, none had heard from their original hometowns, just their adopted city, San Mateo. They pulled out photos and letters from families or from little children who had written them from San Mateo and told me they carried their letters in their pockets to read and re-read several times while in the jungle (they called it "the bush"). It was the only thing that brought them closer to home, and I thought for a moment that a letter carried in a pocket, for some, might have been the last thing that connected them to home or before their young lives were cut short by an enemy bullet, such as Joe's was. The letters mattered. They were love and home and hope.

A few of the boys who knew Joe told me stories about him and recalled how proud he was of me when he received the news article about San Mateo adopting them. "See, I told you my sister would take care of us." The new replacements didn't know Joe but had heard of him and were very appreciative of what he had done for them. That brought tears to my eyes because I was the big sister, always responsible for my younger brothers. But I had let Joe down. But, really, I didn't. I was here now. God sent me to Vietnam to take care of more brothers than I could imagine.

I inquired about identifying the guys who knew Joe the best, and I asked if I could talk to them in private. We walked about 10 feet away from the crowd and sat on a pile of sandbags, where I was offered a warm Pabst Blue Ribbon beer. I don't drink but I took

San Mateo "Adopted Sons" medallion gift

the beer and sipped it to be polite. I asked about Joe and that March day … there was silence. Finally, one started talking, then the others started chiming in, telling me what happened that day.

While their company was on a hunt for the enemy, they discovered a North Vietnamese Army (NVA) stronghold. In the blink of an eye, ABU saw the enemy and attacked and a hellish firefight ensued. One of the men said, "We're the 101st, that's what we do, we attack, attack and attack!"

They told me that as they pushed deeper, the intensity and accuracy of machine gun fire, handheld rockets, and mortars grew greater and greater. Joe's squad was deployed toward the right flank and the intensity of the firefight became even heavier. Automatic weapons fire rained around them, and A Company's casualties mounted. Joe ran through the fire to maneuver the members of his squad. Then Joe turned his attention toward the wounded who were lying in the kill zone. As he attempted to pull his men to safety, he was hit — I didn't need to hear any more. I later learned from the company medic, Doc Tay, that Joe was killed by a sniper instantly.

The Soldiers pointed out that Lieutenant Patterson — their platoon leader and my escort — immediately assaulted the well-concealed, fortified positions to take pressure off the rest of the company. He was hit in the neck but continued to expose himself to automatic weapons fire to maneuver his men. He refused medical aid until all his wounded men were cared for, then was taken by medivac (helicopter) to an area hospital. After getting out of the hospital, he was offered a desk job but he refused and returned to A Company just three weeks later to again lead his men. Joe and Lieutenant Patterson were both awarded the Silver Star that day for their bravery and valor. Although LT Patterson will never tell you, they all said that they would follow Steve, their lieutenant, through the gates of hell. I was speechless but knew what they meant.

It Came Upon the Midnight Clear[14]

The Christmas stand down was a brief three days but was so welcomed by ABU. It meant a shower, clean clothes, hot food, and a cot to rest their weary bodies after a continuous four months in the jungle. Every day, they were on the move humping those mountains.

That evening, there was a Korean band, with always popular go-go dancers, brought in to entertain the troops. I was told that other American entertainers, even Bob Hope, couldn't come up that far north because it was too dangerous. Over the sea of mud from recent monsoon rains was a makeshift stage, a small dance floor and a few rows of benches. The rock-and-roll band began to play, the girls started grinding to Motown songs and of course the GIs roared and yelled. When the guitar player started playing the first few chords of Creedence Clearwater Revival's "Suzie Q,"[15] the Soldiers went wild. I was sitting in the front row, and one Soldier asked me politely if I would dance with him. I said, "Sure, I love Creedence Clearwater!" He pulled me up onto the muddy flat stage, and we started dancing.

Before I knew it, another Soldier tapped on the shoulder of the Soldier I was dancing with, and then another, and then another. Any girl back home would have been green with envy. My dance card was filled with by 110 Soldiers standing in line to dance with me. Yes, even at a young 27, I found myself worn out by these 19-year-olds. A couple of guys got up and starting dancing, doing splits and giving it their all to Wilson Pickett's "Land of 1000 Dances"[16] and "Mustang Sally."[17] I looked on in amazement of their talent.

We had such a great time that evening. For a minute, we all forgot the war. After the band played its last song, LT Patterson walked me over to the Officers Club. It was anything but a club. It was just another makeshift room with a small bar that only had a few beers and soft drinks. We had only been there a few minutes when I heard a group of Soldiers singing "The First Noel."[18] LT Patterson said that the Soldiers were serenading me. I stepped out to hear them, and tears came to my eyes as I looked at their young faces, rugged and worn beyond their years, but as sweet and loving as choir boys as they sang "Silent Night."[19] I held back my tears because it was a moment they gave me, and me alone. So instead of crying, I joined them and sang my heart out.

We heard explosions; it was out-going, LT Patterson assured me, and not to worry. The realization of the war came back ... we were not home ... we were in Vietnam, singing "Silent Night" only a short eight kilometers away from where the war raged on.

> The realization of the war came back ... we were not home ... we were in Vietnam, singing "Silent Night" only a short eight kilometers away from where the war raged on.

Christmas Day 1968

There was a brief but solemn memorial service given by the chaplain for ABU's fallen Soldiers; we sat quietly listening to the sermon. Each name of the fallen was called as if it was a morning roll call; when there was no answer, we prayed for their souls. There was a line of empty boots, upturned M-16s crowned by a steel helmet, then Taps was played. Although Joe had been killed months earlier, they respect-fully included his name for my benefit. All told, A Company would lose more than 30 men killed in action in 1968 and six times that amount that were wounded. Many of the men had been wounded two or three times. A name that was pointed out to

ABU soldiers taking pictures of Linda, Christmas 1968

me was a Lieutenant Meiggs, who would replace LT Patterson as A Company's Executive Officer. LT Meiggs had only minutes left on line — his time in the jungle was almost over and he was headed to become the Executive Officer — when he stepped on a mine. LT Meiggs was Steve's friend. In fact, Steve told me he had picked up a dress for Meiggs's fiancée while he was on his R&R in Hong Kong just a month earlier. I felt the inconceivable pain the Soldiers sitting and standing around me felt each day. How could anyone back home understand their isolated pain and loss, except the families themselves?

Afterwards, we sat around and the ABUs told funny anecdotes about their friends that we had just honored, and eventually our conversation drifted to a Q&A session about home: what the latest fads were, new music, and they wanted to hear all about miniskirts, and more information about their adopted city. They started opening up to me about where they grew up. Many of them were from small towns, so I told them more about San Mateo and how close it was to San Francisco.

The day ended too quickly. Tomorrow would arrive too soon.

Goodbye ABU

The Christmas ceasefire had ended, and it was time for ABU to return to the jungle. LT Patterson picked me up early in the morning and it was the first morning I wasn't running late ... I didn't want to miss saying one single goodbye. At the LZ (Landing Zone) we walked to where the Chinook helicopters were waiting. Captain Shore presented me their guidon, the Regimental 327th flag (a huge honor) and a beautiful plaque: one for the City and one for me. We stood on a little dirt mound with the men and all their gear beside them. They lined up for me, hands reaching out to mine, thanking me one by one. Some gave me the only possessions they had: a Zippo lighter, their paratrooper wings, a 101st pen, a Vietnam headband.

Do you understand how significant that was? They gave me their only possessions. However, what meant the most was that they gave me their hearts and I gave them mine. I smiled and gracefully accepted their tokens and told them "vaya con Dios, Go with God," and "please write." I don't know how I was so composed on the outside, for inside I had completely broken down knowing that, quite possibly, I could be their last touch or look at home. I prayed, asking God to please protect them that night. I will never forget the looks in their eyes — that rare combination of courage and fear. And I'll never forget the warmth of their young hands in mine as they said "thank you, thank you" over and over.

> **I will never forget the looks in their eyes — that rare combination of courage and fear. And I'll never forget the warmth of their young hands in mine as they said "thank you, thank you" over and over.**

The next day, we rose early once again and Steve picked me up. We were heading back to Saigon to catch my flight back home. We were about to say our goodbyes and Steve asked what was wrong. I guess the look in my eyes told him ... leaving was hard for me. In that short time, I had been among "Eagles," and felt so close to them. Something about that moment was clear — we didn't want to say goodbye. And as fate would have it ... I couldn't leave! As I showed my passport at the airport, the Vietnamese government looked at me and said, "Your passport is not stamped entering our Country ... you cannot leave."

"What?" I asked, looking at Steve. Then he said, "Linda, we will have to go to the American Embassy and straighten this out." I looked at him, puzzled, but then remembered that when he whisked me up into that jeep when I first arrived, we never went through customs!

So we went back to nearby Biên Hòa and would have to take care of this another day.

The Commander in charge had Steve put me up in a VIP trailer on the base where I would spend the night. Everything was fine, thank God, and the U.S. Embassy took care of everything so I could leave the next day. Back at Biên Hòa, Steve and I went to the Officers' Club and as we were having a soft drink, a lieutenant with whom Steve had gone through Ranger training came over and introduced himself. He told me he had read about me in the *Stars and Stripes* news article and wondered if I would like to go into Saigon.

I said that sounded nice and I looked at Steve. Steve immediately told the LT that he was my military escort and he would be taking me into Saigon. The LT said fine. Not too happy, it seemed, the other lieutenant walked away.

Chapter 9

Long Ago and Oh So Far Away

That day in Saigon, the heavens opened and so did our eyes. Saigon looked like one huge flea market, buzzing with activity. We walked the streets, looking at the street vendors' stalls that were selling everything imaginable: fish, pork, kitchenware, cigarettes, live chickens, dead frogs, vegetables, and a fish sauce that smelled like … well, use your imagination. I bought a small jacket for my son and little Chinese slippers for my daughter. Then we jumped on a rickshaw and toured the French Quarter, marveling at the colonial buildings from the French-Indochina times.

That day in Saigon, the heavens opened and so did our eyes.

Out of nowhere, the heavens opened with a monsoon downpour. Steve and I jumped off the rickshaw, huddled under a little overhead awning, then ducked into a charming French café for shelter from the pouring rain. The café was in the old French Quarter. There were lit candles on each of the white lace covered tables, overhead ceiling fans were slowly turning and paintings of the French countryside adorned the walls. French music was playing in the background and, except for Steve and me, there was not another soul in the dining area. We sat at a table with a view of the inner courtyard and said nothing as we watched the rain run down the glass panes and the courtyard ferns bend from the monsoon wind. The silence was broken when Steve summoned the waiter and ordered dinner for the two of us, then we both returned to our private thoughts. The theme song from *Moulin Rouge*[20] started playing and, hearing the words, I started humming along. I looked at Steve, and we both fell into each other's eyes.

Love ... Love Is Strange

When the rain let up, we reluctantly took the last sips of our coffees and then found our way back to Biên Hòa and my lavish general's accommodations: a VIP trailer. It was getting dark and looked as if it was going to rain again, so I asked Steve if he wanted to come in. He said that he better not and, as if on cue, it started pouring ... he changed his mind. I gave him a Coke from the fridge, turned on the radio and sat on a chair across from him. Then, for a brief moment, we caught each other eyes again, something funny was happening. I remember telling Steve that the girl who got him would surely be lucky. He laughed.

For the first time we didn't only talk about ABU ... we told each other about ourselves. I began to talk about myself, telling him about Al, and opened up and told him why I had married him. Steve asked, "Linda, do you love Al?" I held my head down and said "no" in a barely audible tone. Still mumbling, I said this trip to Vietnam had opened my eyes. I no longer wanted to lead an unhappy life and I would be going home to get a divorce. We were both quiet for the longest time; when I finally lifted my head, I had to clear my throat twice for Steve to look at me. Steve smiled with his eyes, and motioned for me to sit by him. Again, the gods must have been smiling on us, for at that very moment "This Magic Moment"[21] by the Drifters started playing on the radio.

> *"This magic moment, So different and so new*
> *Was like any other, Until I kissed you*
> *And then it happened, It took me by surprise*
> *I knew that you felt it too, By the look in your eyes*
> *Sweeter than wine, Softer than the summer night*
> *Everything I want I have, Whenever I hold you tight*
> *This magic moment, While your lips are close to mine*
> *Will last forever, forever, 'til the end of time."*

Steve kissed me, or was it me who kissed him? At any rate, it was a long kiss that arose a feeling I had never felt in my life. Steve broke off the kiss and said, "Linda, I love you. I fell in love with you two weeks ago when I first saw you on that hot airport tarmac and you removed your sunglasses."

I answered that I felt the same about him, but that I realized he had not seen or been with a woman in a long time, and that I imagined as soon as he returned to the States he would forget me. No, he assured me, that was not the case. In fact, he would be leaving soon, in just a couple of weeks, and he would come to see me. Everything happened so quickly that evening; it was like a dream for me, and it was the first time in my life that I knew I was in love. I had been secretly attracted to him, not only by his good looks, but because I came to know him. I knew he was special when I listened to his troops tell me that after Steve was wounded, he could have stayed back in the rear with a cushy job but instead chose to go back in the field with his men. The men said he was the best platoon leader they had and that they would march into hell with him. Those words coming from the grunts meant a lot to me.

I thought to myself how lucky it would be for a girl to have him by her side the rest of her life. Steve explained that to him, the last couple of weeks of always being by my side was like marathon dating for months. I knew exactly what he meant; I felt the same. That evening was heaven, no better way to describe it, two people brought together by war, hopelessly in love.

Tomorrow I'll Miss You[22]

During the night, there had been a guard posted at my door. I was horrified that they would find out that Steve spent the night with me. Steve said it would be OK and that once the guard left, he would go get us breakfast. He returned with coffee, juice, donuts and news that the base commander requested to meet me before I left. After coffee and a short conversation with the base commander, the general ordered a military taxi instead of a jeep to take us to the airport. Steve and I sat in back of the taxi holding hands discreetly, not wanting anyone to see our affections for one another.

After checking in with the airline, Steve stayed with me until it was time to board. I gave him a hug and said goodbye, and he promised that he would see me in a few short weeks. As I was climbing the stairs to the plane, I looked back and saw Steve standing at a window looking at me. I smiled, waved and then became very despondent thinking about what had happened and wondering if I would ever see him again. My heart ached to leave him in Saigon, knowing that he was going back in-country to Camp Eagle. I prayed to God to please keep him safe, and bring him home to me soon.

Chapter 10
Back in the World

Flashbacks

During the long flight back, I mentally reviewed my Vietnam odyssey. Thousands of images danced behind my eyelids each time I closed my eyes. Oh, how I missed my ABUs. What would or could I say to the people of San Mateo about my visit with the 101st that could have the same impact to them in the hearing as it had on my life by actually being there? What it meant to be upfront and close to the war. How could I convey in just words what I had seen, felt and experienced in that short period of time? Would I touch their hearts like those young paratroopers touched mine? Sadly, I knew that once home I would look upon the Roster lists with updates of new troop replacements from Company A, I'd see names that I recognized — young men I had met — which would make me smile, and that I'd also see names lined through. with "KIA" (Killed in Action) or Wounded written beside them. Each time, it would break my heart and a little more of me would die. As painful as it was, I had to carry on as I knew they had. Goodbye, my brothers. Today, my tears are for you.

In between these thoughts, I kept thinking of Steve. I had not expected it to happen, but it did. How did I fall so deeply in love with a Soldier I had known only two weeks? I wondered if Joe had a hand in it and then I thought maybe it was God's gift to me.

Turn the Page[23]

My flight home to San Francisco landed late at night, and even though my family and friends were notified of my delay returning, there was no one to meet me. I took a taxi home and let myself in. Al was passed out on the living room couch with an empty bottle at his side. Tomorrow, tomorrow I will tell him I want out of this love-less marriage. I told myself that Steve had nothing to do with this, that I wanted out of this marriage ... desperately, long before I went to Vietnam. Al was not surprised to hear that I wanted a divorce immediately upon my return; he knew before I left how unhappy I was. He again promised to change his drinking habits, but he knew it was too late and that I didn't love him. The Cotchett law firm was upstairs from my office, which seemed fortuitous. On my first day back at work, I made an appointment with Joe Cotchett and asked how quickly I could get a divorce. He told me it would take at least six months. He filed the divorce papers for me that very day.

Express Yourself[24]

Next on my agenda was my report to the San Mateo City Council. I stood before them and tried to express what my visit meant to our adopted Soldiers, and how I had changed in just those two short weeks with them. I tried to convey the character of our troopers — how proud they were of their unit, but moreover how they fought for one another, willing to die for a brother beside them. They fought hard, and were quick to point out that they had won their battles, contrary to what the news media reported. They were only doing the job that they were asked to do — why did the people back home blame them for this war? With these thoughts, I remembered President Kennedy's words, "Ask not what your country can do for you, but what you can do for your country."

Every one of these courageous men — 18, 19, 20 and older — were doing that very thing while students their age at home were burning draft cards, our flag and carrying signs calling them baby killers. I wondered how Americans years later would look upon that scene. Would they mourn for the young Soldiers who died an ocean away, or would that pain only remain with the brave men who survived, and with the families of the fallen? Would America eventually welcome them home, as San Mateo was prepared to do? I told my Mayor and Council that, more than ever, we need to continue our support for them and they agreed.

I presented the City with the mementos that I was asked to carry back: the plaque, the 327th guidon and, most importantly, their words of thanks and appreciation from the bottom of their hearts. I thanked the Council for the special Christmas gift I had been given by the City of San Mateo, an experience no other everyday American woman had ever experienced. I had been honored by the 327th to be called their sister, but mostly I had been given the gift to stand tall among Eagles. San Mateo listened and acted.

Chapter 11

Ain't No Sunshine When You're Gone[25]

The Power of Prayer

I had been home from Vietnam a week, and every day at lunch
I would go to a nearby Catholic church and kneel before the Virgin
Mary and ask her to please keep Steve from harm's way, and to send
him to me. At the end of the second week, I returned to my office
from lunch late. My boss, Ron Wright, said that I had been getting
calls from a Lieutenant Steve Patterson — that he was at Travis
airport and wanted to see me. *"Oh my God, did I hear that right?"*
I asked myself. *"Mother Mary have you answered my prayers?"*

Steve called again and we wanted so desperately for us to see each
other. He insisted on taking a taxi from Travis all the way to San
Mateo and asked where we should meet. I told him to have the cab
take him to San Bruno and that there was a corner coffee shop called
Lyons, on El Camino, and that I would be waiting for him there.
I couldn't wait! After work, I raced to San Bruno. When I saw him
in the parking lot, we ran to each other and, yes, it was just like in
the movies. We drove out to Half Moon Bay and walked the beach

together and found a small cave where we watched the waves and talked about our future together. Steve stayed in San Mateo two weeks, Chief Noe Chanteloup put him up in a hotel room and I took him around to visit everyone: *The San Mateo Times*, the Mayor, and Barbara Schroeder and her family (by now I had told her about my relationship with Steve).

Steve in dress greens on
his first night home

Everyone was aware that I was getting a divorce and wondered why it took me so long. It seems they all knew of Al's drinking and never thought he was good for me. On the other hand, everyone who met Steve fell in love with him. His parents called him from New York and could not understand why it was taking him so long to return to their home in Massapequa. Finally, he told them that he had met someone and wanted them to meet me. He told them how we met and what I was doing, but he did not tell them I was in the process of a divorce or that I had children. Steve told me that his parents came from a devout Italian/Greek Catholic family and that they needed to meet me before learning all the details. He assured me they too would fall in love with me. Steve finally had to leave for home, so we said goodbye and he left San Mateo for New York. And I waited.

Meet the Pattersons

Only hours after arriving home, Steve called and said he wanted me to come out and meet his parents as soon as I could catch a flight. I knew I would be gone for some time so I called my ABU co-chairwoman Barbara Schroeder and asked if she would take over in my absence. Barbara was the only one I could trust to keep the support going. She agreed then asked when I would return. I said in a few months because Steve wanted his parents to get to know me before he told them that I was divorced with two small children. I explained that he came from a strong Catholic family and they wouldn't understand. But, if they just had a chance to meet me, they would grow to love me, and it would be easier to explain my present situation. I had agreed, but it meant that my children would have to stay with my grandmother for an undetermined period of time. It wasn't easy for me to do that, but I knew it would be just for a short time.

I gave my notice at work and began to wrap up my life in San Mateo as I prepared to go to New York to be with Steve. The day before I left, my best friend Linda Takenouchi and I went to see Barbara Streisand's latest movie *Funny Girl*. Watching that movie, I related to Streisand's character and because the movie was filmed in New York City, I couldn't wait to leave to see it for myself. The excitement of running to the love of my life, Steve, in New York was bursting out of me. Watching Streisand on screen singing "Don't Rain on my Parade"[26] struck a chord with me — nothing would stand in my way of being with the man of my dreams. New York, New York here I come! My life was just beginning, my bags were packed and I had my ticket that Steve had sent for me. I had a new life ahead and knew what happiness felt like for the first time in my life. My heart raced watching Streisand sing that nothing was going to stand in her way to be with her love, as I was about to do. I got lost in her character. I'm a born romantic.

> *"Get ready for me, love,*
> *Cause I'm a comer,*
> *I simply gotta march,*
> *My heart's a drummer.*
> *Nobody, no, nobody*
> *Is gonna rain on my parade!"*

My friend Linda saw me off at the San Francisco Airport and wished me happiness. I trusted her with what would be my new address in New York. No, I didn't tell my mother.

Steve's parents were great! They were every bit of what I had always dreamed a family should be like. As soon as I arrived, they planned a party for all the family to meet me. They wanted to amaze and surprise everyone with the story of how we'd met. Steve had already proposed marriage to me back in San Mateo and, of course, I had accepted — after all, he was what I had dreamt about and he was my dream come true. We had an official engagement party thrown by his family members in Brooklyn and we began planning our wedding. I knew I had to return to San Mateo soon ... I missed my children terribly. I felt awful not telling Steve's parents from the very beginning that I wasn't the young single girl they saw me as but was a mother. The guilt of leaving my kids was tearing at my heart, but Steve just wanted to wait a little longer to break the news. I remember going into his sister's bedroom closet and sobbing uncontrollably because I missed my children so much. I wanted it all to work out for *all* of us, but it was so hard.

The day came when we sat his family down and told them the truth. It was gut-wrenching to break the news to Steve's parents about my children. Of course, their immediate reaction was shock and confusion. There was lots of crying on my part, trying to make them understand my love for their son. I remember his mother sitting on the bed, telling me, "Linda, try to understand how we feel." Their only son — she didn't have to say it but I thought I could read her thoughts: a divorcée with two children ... this is not what they had hoped for, I'm sure. I remember his mom telling me, "Linda, if it is meant to be, God willing, it will be ..."

"Linda, if it is meant to be, God willing, it will be ..."

And, just as Steve had predicted, they understood and accepted our relationship — and me — after getting to know me. At this point, I had to leave Steve once again. He was beginning his chosen career — training as a stockbroker — and needed to finish up training with a brokerage firm. It was time for me to go back to California to my children, where he would follow in six months.

Getting settled into a new routine as a single woman with two kids was not easy. At first, I stayed with my dad in San Jose and put the kids in school while I looked for work to help pay our way. I couldn't wait to get back up to San Mateo where Barbara was eager for me to pick up where I had left off. A few months later, I was able to move back, thanks to Noe Chanteloup who got me bumped up on a waiting list for the San Mateo Hillsdale Garden Apartments. Steve would soon be joining us. I longed for his phone calls and would love hearing his plans for the two of us, always encouraging me to "keep the faith" in his letters. I held on to his every word and knew the power of love would make everything right.

As promised, Steve joined me and the kids six months later. He had everything planned out, wrapped up his job at the brokerage firm and told his parents he needed to be with me in California. Steve had saved enough money to help me and the kids, and to also get his own apartment in San Mateo close by. He got a terrific job in San Francisco with the investment banking firm of Glore Forgan Staats on California Street in the newly erected Bank of America Building. We were together and that was all that mattered.

We were together and that was all that mattered.

Our plans for getting married were on hold for a while. I had faith in his every word, and he wanted to plan ahead so we would have something when we would marry. He was constantly with me outside of work — coming to my apartment for dinner, playing with the kids (who craved a great father figure like Steve and immediately loved him!), and watching the late-night show, then, like clockwork, he would return to his own apartment. We would meet every morning at our favorite coffee shop called "Loves" — can you imagine the irony of that name?

We were both busy working by this time. I had landed a job as the legal secretary to the Head Legal Counsel at the California Teachers Association and, as the war continued, I continued my work with the Adopted Sons program. I realized that Steve wanted to put the war behind him, but I was always there — talking about the ABUs, sending letters and care packages — so I learned to do things without him. The 101st was his past, but it was my present. If I was asked to speak at some club or other civic organization, I would use my lunch-break or whatever free time I had. I had to respect Steve's feelings and his needs. Our love was strong, but deep down he knew he had to share that other love I had for the troops. It would always be there, and I couldn't let go until we brought them home. He accepted it but kept his distance. Throughout his life, Steve battled the demons of post-traumatic stress disorder (PTSD) and only felt comfortable with the men he FOUGHT with. The years went on ... '69, '70, '71 and finally '72.

Homeward Bound

With me back in San Mateo once again, Barbara and I worked together for ABU as the war continued. Soldiers would rotate home on an individual basis through the San Francisco Airport (SFO), where Barbara and I would see that they were picked up and taken to the Villa Hotel in San Mateo. Joe Greenback, who co-owned the hotel with his brother, had agreed to arrange a room for any of our Soldiers who were visiting before traveling to their respective hometowns. Many elected to stay with us for three or four days. Once arriving at the Villa Hotel, there would be champagne and flowers welcoming them home on behalf of the people of San Mateo. They then would be given an escorted tour of their "adopted city." They were introduced to Vera Graham at *The San Mateo Times*. You will recall her as the reporter who had written so many great articles about our "Adopted Sons" and the one who had printed the letters they had written to us from Vietnam as an "Open Letter" to the people of the City.

While in town, our Screaming Eagles met the Mayor and City Council members as well. Many of the returning troops particularly enjoyed meeting Chief Noe and the firemen, who cooked for them. The troops loved the firemen and, in fact, some preferred to bunk down at the fire station and hang out with the firefighters. Noe would often take them out for a good meal as well. On one occasion, I remember a young 19-year-old ABU dining with us. We were sitting at the Lyon's Restaurant Club/Bar in the back. Noe had ordered a beer for the young man and the waitress said, "Sir, I need to see his I.D." Noe looked at her and said, "Lady, this kid just came in from Vietnam from fighting a war. You give him a beer, I'll be responsible, OK?" I'll never forget the look on the face of that young underaged kid who was old enough to fight a war, watch his buddies die and answer a call of duty by his country but not old enough to buy a beer. He smiled from ear to ear and said, "Thank you, sir" to Noe, who just smiled back and said "No ... thank *you*, son!"

For the most part, our Soldiers wanted to meet the families who had written to them. They carried the pictures of the family or children who wrote to them in Vietnam. Many had their first home-cooked meal with their "Adopted Families." This was San Mateo's way of saying thank you for all they'd done for us, their sacrifices and their service to our country. No demonstrators were to be found marching in San Mateo. Instead, they were greeted with hugs, handshakes and home-cooked meals. Sometimes we would have a local beauty queen, Miss San Mateo, take them to dinner at the Villa Chartier, which was an exotic restaurant that welcomed them with a free dinner for two. Those who were able to visit San Mateo couldn't believe the reception they received. One such Soldier, Bob Chambers who was from New Jersey, later moved his wife and small baby son out to San Mateo. Bob Chambers had written a very powerful letter to San Mateo, and Vera had published it in *The Times* on May 22, 1968. His letter made the people very much aware of what our Soldiers, our City's adopted sons, were faced with on a day-to-day basis.

* * *

HOW LIFE IS FOR ADOPTED TROOPERS
Wednesday, May 22, 1968, *The San Mateo Times*

A personal letter of thanks to all San Mateo area residents who have sent letters and gifts to adopted company "A" of the "Screaming Eagles" 101st Airborne Division in Vietnam was received today.

Wednesday, May 22, 1968   The Times   San Mateo—27

How Life Is For Adopted Troopers

A personal letter of thanks to all San Mateo area residents who have sent letters and gifts to adopted company "A" of the "Screaming Eagles" of the 101st Airborne Division in Vietnam was received today. It stated:

Dear San Mateans:

I wish to convey my gratitude to the people of San Mateo and the organizations and individuals responsible for the enthusiastic support offered "A" company of our battalion. We sure can use it.

A little about your adopted company. It is situated approximately 20 miles west of Hue, blocking the A Shau Valley, at his writing.

The men spend nearly all of their 12 months tour on line, fighting or hunting the enemy. They come in from the field unshaven, filthy, tired, miserable, and eager for packages, mail, a cold drink etc. After three or four days of this, they return for another operation with little pomp or circumstance. We see them again only if they are wounded, evacuated for malaria or other tropical maladies or are coming in for R & R or rotation to the States. After four to eight weeks of fighting this takes place again, and so it goes.

Its been this way since July of 65.

We take an odd sense of pride in it. You see, few outfits in Vietnam stay in the field, hunting the enemy on extended operations as long as we, nor do they wear the ominous rucksack weighing as much as 60 lbs.

We received $55 per month extra for this grind and are called paratroopers. For many this is compensation enough.

There is also a company roster enclosed with this package. I made it out last night — today of the men I indicated are dead and 17 were wounded. It will be necessary to continuously send you updated rosters for mailing purposes.

We arrived in Vietnam in 1965. The First Brigade is a very proud unit and all of its members would be quick to point out its excellent combat record in the Republic of Vietnam, as a strike force. Wherever a large concentration of North Vietnamese or Viet Cong insurgents are located we are picked up and sped to that location.

The First Brigade is one of the Army's major maneuver elements and we feel the hardest hitting. Intercepted enemy correspondence has verified our self-bias. They often warn each others units of our presence and often stay clear of us. I must admit I wish they would spread the word a little more than they have lately.

Another item of possible interest to you is the typical paratroopers shunning of the word "soldier." He enjoys being called a paratrooper or referred to as "airborne." We go through quite a bit of dangerous training to wear our parachute wings and jump boots.

I wish to inform you of these prevailing attitudes for the sole purpose of producing a harmonious and understanding relationship between the people of San Mateo and the paratroopers of "A" Company.

Last of all, anything to make these guys feel welcomed, relayed entertained, and glad to be back in the States. The world press is rather critical, and insinuations and name-calling filters across the Pacific to these tormented jungles we daily fight for.

These guys have spent one heck of a rough year. "A" Company is strictly front line infantry troop. Many have learned to harden their hearts to bear the agony and suffering caused by the frequent deaths of their buddies.

They deserve kindness and consideration. They like to appear tough and often refer to each other as "Hard Core" they are, but any "softening" process you would care to extend to them would be great for their morale, and well-being. Please remember these troopers could take great benefit in having a home-town away from home.

I wish to apologize for handwriting this. You see, we have no typewriter at this time. So anything other than Inter-Army Correspondence, I'm pretty informal out of necessity. My Public Information Office is really a home made desk and a rusty filing cabinet, setting on a dirt floor in a shrapnel torn tent.

But I'm the lucky one. I could be living off the shelter I carry on my back and daily fighting.

for my life as your adopted "A" Company must.

Thanks again for all your interest, Robert A. Chambers, Sgt. Inf.

Article from *The San Mateo Times*, May 22, 2968

Dear San Mateans,

I wish to convey my gratitude to the people of San Mateo, the organizations and individuals responsible for the enthusiastic support offered "A" Company of our battalion. We sure can use it.

A little about your adopted Company. It is situated approximately 20 miles southwest of Huế, blocking the A Shau Valley, as of this writing. The men spend nearly all of their 12-month tour on line, fighting and hunting down the enemy. They come in from the field unshaven, filthy, tired, miserable, and eager for packages, mail, a cold drink etc. After three or four days of this, they return for another operation with little pomp or circumstance. We see them again only if they are wounded, evacuated for malaria or other tropical maladies, or are coming in for R & R or rotation to the States. After three to five months of fighting, this takes place again and so it goes. They get maybe ten days of rest the entire year.

It's been this way since July of '65.

We take an odd sense of pride in it. You see, few if any outfits in Vietnam stay in the field, hunting the enemy on extended operations as long as we, nor do they wear the ominous rucksack weighing as much as 120 lbs.

We received $55 per month extra for this grind and are called paratroopers. For many, this is compensation enough.

There is also a company roster enclosed with this package. I made it out last night — today three of the men I indicated are dead and 17 were wounded. It will be necessary to continuously send you updated rosters for mailing purposes.

We arrived in Vietnam in 1965. The First Brigade is a very proud unit and all of its members would be quick to point out its excellent combat record in the Republic of Vietnam as a strike force.

Wherever a large concentration of North Vietnamese or Viet Cong insurgents are located, we are picked up and speed to that location.

The First Brigade is one of the Army's major maneuver elements and we feel the hardest hitting. Intercepted enemy correspondence has verified our self-bias. They often warn each other's units of our presence and often stay clear of us. I must admit I wish they would spread the word a little more than they have lately.

Another item of possible interest to you is the typical paratrooper's shunning of the word "Soldier." He enjoys being called a paratrooper or referred to as "airborne." We go through quite a bit of dangerous training to wear our parachute wings and jump boots.

I wish to inform you of these prevailing attitudes for the sole purpose of producing a harmonious and understanding relationship between the people of San Mateo and the paratroopers of "A" Company.

Last of all, anything to make these guys feel welcomed, relayed entertained, and glad to be back in the States. The world press is rather critical, and insinuations and name-calling filters across the Pacific to these tormented jungles we daily fight for.

These guys have spent one hell of a rough year. "A" Company is strictly a frontline infantry troop. Many have learned to harden their hearts to bear the agony and suffering caused by the frequent deaths of their buddies.

They deserve kindness and consideration. They like to appear tough and often refer to each other as "Hard Core," they are, but any softening process you would care to extend to them would be great for their morale, and well-being. Please remember these troopers could take great benefit in having a hometown away from home. I wish to apologize for handwriting this. You see, we have no typewriter at this time. So anything other than Inter-Army Correspondence, I'm pretty informal out of necessity. My Public Information Office is really a homemade desk and a rusty filing cabinet, setting on a dirt floor in a shrapnel-torn tent.

But I'm the lucky one. I could be living off the shelter I carry on my back and daily fighting for my life as your adopted "A" Company must.

Thanks again for all your interest,
Robert A. Chambers, SGT Inf.

* * *

I remember thinking how strange it was to watch the countless demonstrations of anti-war protesters burning the American flag or their draft cards on TV. Hearing marchers chant, "Hey, Hey, LBJ how many kids did you kill today?" Whether or not it was intentional, the anti-war movement often felt decidedly "anti-Soldier." It was important that we properly welcome these troops home, especially after just receiving a letter like this from Soldiers who explained that they believed there was a corner in "The World" (as they referred to the United States) where the people seemed to care about them. It seemed incongruous to me that the rest of the nation couldn't see and embrace our military as we had done in San Mateo. I wanted our Veterans to feel the shower of love that they felt from San Mateo from *every* city in the United States. They were our own sons returning home to us. Their letters expressed to us, their "adopted family," what they were feeling ... feelings they couldn't even write to their own families. It was the letters from us that carried the spirit and affection of San Mateans to them in those torrid jungles.

As always, Barbara and I couldn't wait to call each other when we got a letter, reading it to each other over the phone. We shared our news from our adopted sons with each other, our families, our friends, our supporters and read the letters aloud at civic clubs ... always with our audiences, in the end, asking, "How can we help?"

> It seemed incongruous to me that the rest of the nation couldn't see and embrace our military as we had done in San Mateo.

The Sweet, Sweet Sound of Your Voice

Always searching for new ways to raise morale, I borrowed a tape recorder, I think it was a Wollensak, from a local camera shop to tape the sounds and voices of home for our Soldiers. I set off the next morning with the tape recorder and saw some city construction workers breaking ground. Amid the rat-tat-tat, I said, "Excuse me, would you guys like to send a message to our troops in Vietnam?" "Sure lady, I have a nephew and a brother over there." The next stop was *The San Mateo Times* newsroom, hearing the sounds of the presses running at the newspaper was pretty cool! Reporters who had worked so hard to keep the community aware of our adopted sons were next on my recorder. Today, instead of writing, they would talk into that little microphone and tell our adopted sons how PROUD we were of them. I was getting some great stuff when I thought of the kids! So I packed up my recorder and hastened off to a local elementary school. I caught a teacher in the hall who had a kindergarten class, into which she invited me. One by one, her boys and girls spoke, in their sweet voices, "I hope you all can come home soon ... kill the bad guys and Merry Christmas."

Chapter 12

The Times They Are a-Changin'[27]

And the Beat Goes On ...[28]

Suddenly, we found ourselves mired in the turbulent '70s, part of the "Me Generation." The war in Southeast Asia continued and there was no escaping it. The news media spouted hateful words and attitudes at the military and the government — seemingly with glee — and often painted the war protestors in a sympathetic light. Radio stations broadcast the songs of the day:

"Ball of Confusion" by The Temptations[29]

"War (What Is It Good For?) by Edwin Starr[30]

"For What It's Worth" by Buffalo Springfield[31]

"Turn! Turn! Turn! (To Everything There Is a Season) by The Byrds[32]

We were struck by the haunting lyrics from "Where Have All the Flowers Gone" by Peter, Paul and Mary ...

"Where have all the Soldiers gone, long time passing?
Where have all the Soldiers gone, long time ago?
Where have all the Soldiers gone?
Gone to graveyards, every one.
Oh, when will they ever learn?
Oh, when will they ever learn?"[33]

And Dylan sang "The Times They Are a-Changin'"[34] ... and they were. The turbulent '70s. The Wonder Years ... it's a wonder we survived them.

We were awash with emotion and change. Oddly, we were as carefree as we were overwhelmed. Our passions and activities took us to both ends of the emotional spectrum. It was a dizzying time.

For those of you who are too young, let me offer you a glimpse of your parents' (or grandparents') lives. It wasn't all love-ins, paisleys, flower power, bell-bottom jeans, rock concerts and painted vans. History shows you the sentiment of the country by holding up to the camera those who were making the loudest noise, but does not show you the core of the men fighting the war in Vietnam and what they faced daily in those torrid jungles. History conveniently says little about why our Soldiers were mystified as to the reasons America turned its back on them. They were only doing their job, doing what our country asked them to do. All they had was each other. Ask anyone of them today and they will tell you they fought for each other. This ethos was hardly reflective of the "Me Generation" that was in full force back at home.

> **History conveniently says little about why our Soldiers were mystified as to the reasons America turned its back on them. They were only doing their job, doing what our country asked them to do.**

Perhaps the gravity of what our Soldiers were facing was hard to understand for Americans sitting at home with their comforts and daily lives — and especially those college students who used their campus forums for spouting speeches calling our Soldiers baby killers and worse. But what happened at home reached across the ocean. Those "words" struck like a sword. The protest signs and the sense that there was an "us and them" divide between civilians and servicemen ... our men on the ground in Vietnam had plenty of time, marching through jungles and being shot at, to think about the country that seemed to have forgotten them or, worse, to be blaming them for the horrors of war.

We in San Mateo knew all too well the disconnect between much of the nation and the men fighting to protect it. Many of the letters we received from our Screaming Eagles told us why San Mateo meant so much to them. It wasn't the politics of the war they were struggling with; it was about why so many Americans seemed to have turned on them (or forgotten them). Some of them felt the need to remove their uniforms upon returning home, fearing they'd be shunned and criticized rather than embraced and thanked. Had they not earned their medals with valor like their fathers before them? Didn't they serve proudly as their nation had asked? They wondered what it would be like coming home. They'd heard rumors that Soldiers might be shouted at or about, or even spat upon, once they stepped off what they referred to as a "Freedom Bird" (i.e., a civilian airplane) and greeted by protestors blaming them for the war.

Vietnam — "We Gotta Get Out of This Place"[35]

Mid-year 1971. Talk was in the air that President Nixon would be withdrawing American troops from Vietnam and that the last coming home would be our 101st Airborne Division, our famed Screaming Eagles. Oh my God! Barbara, Chief Noe Chanteloup and

I realized it was our chance to bring our "Adopted Sons" home to receive the homecoming they deserved and were promised. The City Officials and the Mayor were thrilled. If we could pull this off with U.S. Army support, it would be the homecoming our paratroopers deserved. It would need a lot of planning and coordinating to bring the entire "ABU Company" — 130 Soldiers — straight from Vietnam to San Mateo.

I wrote to U.S. Secretary of Defense Melvin Laird, asking permission to bring our unit to San Mateo for the homecoming we had promised. We received a positive response and so the planning began. Chief Chanteloup was appointed by Mayor Condon to Chair the Homecoming Committee and Barbara and I were appointed as Co-Chairmen. As Chief of the Fire Department, Noe knew everyone in the community, including business and civic leaders, all of whom were willing to help. A few of the Soldiers' families, mothers and sisters planned to join us in San Mateo from all across the country for the festivities. But time would be tight. We had a short three months to pull it all together.

Local press releases energized San Mateans; everyone stepped up to do their part. The planning stages took off like wildfire. "Homecoming Badges" were made and sold to raise funds, while the Army coordinated the day of arrival. Parade arrangements were made to include school and military bands, local participants, equestrian groups, and even the Scottish Black Watch (also known as the Highland Regiment) was eager to take part. The Villa Hotel was ready to roll out the red carpet and house our troops during their stay. We would have them for three glorious days!

The countdown began three months before January 22, 1972 — the big day when San Mateo's Adopted Sons would arrive via one-way tickets from Vietnam to their adopted home, San Mateo, California, USA! Meetings were held at City Hall for the homecoming committee

and, like Chief Chanteloup had promised, we would give them
a homecoming they would never forget!

We would give them a homecoming they would never forget!

The San Mateo Times kept everyone in the community updated
with our progress. People began to call in, "Can we have one of our
adopted sons for a good, old-fashioned, home-cooked meal at our
house?" Names were given out and people were thrilled! Our troops
would be part of the parade given in their honor. The ABUs asked if
it would be okay to march in their jungle fatigues, letting the people
know they were fighters in the "Best Unit" and, after all, they were the
Screaming Eagles. Yes, yes, yes!

Finally, the day came, and
emotions were running
high, especially for me
after four years of intense
support. We lined up in
front of the Villa Hotel:
City Mayor John Condon,
City Council members,
Chief Noe Chanteloup,
the current Miss San
Mateo, Barbara and me
— all with our stretched

Mayor John Condon (SM) and Miss San Mateo
welcoming adopted sons home from war

arms to welcome them home as the buses rolled in.

As our troops got off the buses, some couldn't believe their eyes
when they saw their mothers or other family members waiting in the
crowd. Tears flowed, and smiles, so many smiles (from and for the
young men) beamed on every face. Soldiers, hardcore you bet, but
with softening expressions you could see in their eyes, disbelieving

what they were experiencing in this City called San Mateo. They had been prepared to expect anything. Everything was what they got!

Linda welcoming soldiers home, January 1972

The parade would take place the next day. Members of the media — from all over — showed up after hearing about a town in California where, contrary to America's national sentiments of apathy or disdain, took a different turn toward our warriors coming home. We were hosting a true welcome home, not just for one or two servicemen but for an entire unit. And we were celebrating not just for a day, but for three days of red-carpet welcome. After all, our ABU sons were our VIPs and San Mateo was determined to welcome them as such!

It was a cold January morning but that didn't stop people from lining the streets to cheer and applaud as our Eagles marched by. Everyone seemed to be waving American flags and everyone was thanking them. My children sat alongside the dignitaries at the parade grandstand, celebrating with us all. You could hear yells of "Thank you for your service" ... and that gratitude really meant something!!!

At the 1972 homecoming, a Soldier gives his helmet and jacket to a young boy

The parade ended in San Mateo's Central Park, where our Soldiers listened to a few speeches and then dropped out of formation to enjoy a barbeque, where Soldiers and citizens could meet and mingle. And this was where the most heartwarming thing happened. Soldiers removed their helmets and uniform jackets and gave them to the kids in the park. The kids loved it!! Some of those Soldiers threw the kids on their shoulders and walked around the park. One police officer said that this was something he had experienced with his father coming home from WWII. Homes across San Mateo put out their welcome mats and many families took their individual Soldiers into San Francisco for a day of touring, showing them Fishermen's Wharf, the North Beach clubs, and as much as they could cram into the day. It was a whirlwind, and a far cry from the rigors of warfare. For the 101st Airborne, their first taste of peace was celebratory and heartfelt.

Press clippings from the 1972 homecoming march

Press clipping about the 1972 homecoming parade and ceremony
with a list of Soldiers and their home towns

The following evening, a formal dinner banquet was held at the Villa Hotel, where speeches where delivered and tokens of appreciation were given to the City from the officers and men. The troops had brought a large painting of Vietnam depicting American Soldiers joined with South Vietnam Soldiers (ARVN). It was at that moment that the Mayor proclaimed that San Mateo would erect a permanent home for all our gifts, artifacts, letters, photos and memorabilia — to be displayed in perpetuity within the City's main public library for all to see. Mayor Condon asked me to form a committee to lead this effort. I called our committee and our goal "the Screaming Eagles Memorial Room." It would take us two years to complete and would be our next labor of love.

On the last day of our three-day Welcome Home celebration, we gave our Eagles a farewell breakfast. With fondness, I recalled what a monumental task it was to put together this series of events. We'd done it all in three short months and that had ended all too soon. *"Goodbye ABU,"* I remember thinking. *"May your young lives be blessed as you move on."*

General Wright and Linda, 1972 San Mateo Adopted Sons homecoming

Chapter 13

He Ain't Heavy, He's My Brother[36] – Peace with Honor

President Richard Nixon announced at a news conference on Midway Island in 1969 that the United States involvement in the Vietnam War was coming to an end as a result of a plan that had been instituted. Nixon said that the United States would be following a new program he termed "Vietnamization." Under the provisions of this program, South Vietnamese forces would be built up so they could assume more responsibility for the war. As the South Vietnamese forces became more capable, U.S. forces would be withdrawn from combat and returned to the United States.

President Nixon kept his word and in 1972, America's war in Vietnam was over. Our combat troops came home. "Peace with Honor." They did their job. They won their battles against a determined enemy. They made their sacrifices with a large cost of more than 58,000 American lives. They deserved to come home to a grateful Nation. But, by and large, that was not to be. The exception? One American City — San Mateo, California.

> "Peace with Honor." They did their job. They won their battles against a determined enemy. They made their sacrifices with a large cost of more than 58,000 American lives. They deserved to come home to a grateful Nation.

After our remarkable and historic three-day celebration to welcome home our adopted sons, it was time to do even more to honor them. San Mateo Mayor John Condon wanted to publicly display the honor and affection the community held for the young warriors we called our "adopted sons," men we looked upon as the finest and bravest Soldiers. The Screaming Eagles Memorial Room had been announced at the welcome home banquet, and now our work began. The location would be in the San Mateo Public Library's Main Library and the room would take two years to build.

It was an emotional journey, because so much love had passed between Soldiers and citizens. during those four and a half years. Countless Soldiers had visited San Mateo as their first stop on their DEROS home (i.e., the date they were eligible to return from overseas and end their "tour of duty"). And then the final 130 paratroopers who attending the final homecoming for the Unit shared so many memories with our city. There had been a continuous exchange of countless letters, pictures, memorabilia and cherished mementos shared between an elite military unit and a civilian populace who had kept their promise to SGT Joe Artavia, who pleaded "If you would adopt us, our 'Morale would rise higher than the Clouds.'" These were his last words written home.

The exhibit at the library told our story with wall and table displays, much like a museum. We sorted through the years of endearing letters, photos and artifacts that would be publicly displayed. Each artifact was proof that the affections of a city and its people for the men who we accepted as our "adopted sons and heroes" was real and enduring and truly mattered.

My brother Joe's mission carried beyond what he had expected. In my heart, he has been and continues to be the spiritual force behind the mission he laid down for us. So, very carefully, I formed a committee of genuine and truly compassionate patriots to oversee every letter incased and every photo enlarged to tell the story for generations to come. We brought in a professional curator who would come to our meetings to consult and assist. His time, as well as all others who served on the Screaming Eagles Memorial Room project, was pro bono. Interestingly enough, a young Vietnam Vet showed up at one of our meetings. His name was Roy Hansen and he had strong features, was a bit rough around the edges, and wanted to help us and be part of our committee. We were thrilled to have him! Roy turned out to be very valuable, advising us and making suggestions for each niche on the wall. At times, Roy would become AWOL and I would beg him to come back. Like many combat Veterans, he had deeply rooted issues dealing with the war. He would disappear for a short time but, sure enough, he would show up at another meeting and we all took a sigh of relief knowing how valuable Roy was to us and knowing he was doing well enough to join us again.

We sent out a call through *Army* magazine for any related items to be donated for our exhibit. The outpouring of support in the form of treasured possessions was heartwarming and overwhelming. With the thousands of items we gathered, we probably could have used a warehouse. Our designated space on the library's third floor had niches all around the walls and, of course, there were bookcases. We had to accept the fact that it was, after all a library, but we made the most of it. It came together as if God had a hand in it. Toward the end of the room, in the last niche, was a special painting of our fallen Soldiers making that last march ... Joe among them. I will never forget a local artist by the name of Richard, whose art studio was called

"Poor Richard," approached me and said he would do a painting for our fallen Soldiers and produced a hauntingly beautiful piece of his genius art that we placed prominently in the room. It depicts the sadly endless line of our fallen, marching into heaven, watched over by one lone Soldier standing by a tree. He told me he sketched out a Soldier with a rucksack on his back and told me that was Joe. Compiling that Memorial room was a labor of love that began in 1972 after the ABUs' homecoming and was completed in 1974.

Poor Richard's "Soldiers to Heaven" painting

It came together as if God had a hand in it.

The Committee announced that we were ready to declare the Screaming Eagle Memorial Room open with a public dedication ceremony on August 9, 1974. The City Council was excited and helped get the word out via local news media announcements. Invitations were sent out to all

From left to right: MAJ General John Cushman, General Maxwell Taylor, Linda, LT General Melvin Zais and CSM Michael Collins

government offices and organizations that had a personal connection over the years: police and fire departments, schools, civic clubs, local businesses, places of worship and more. The 101st Division Commander, General John Cushman, planned to come out from Fort Campbell, Kentucky, for the ceremony with a gift for the City to be placed in the Screaming Eagles Memorial Room. His gift was a handwritten scroll with 20,000 individual Soldier's signatures ... thanking San Mateo.

The big day arrived for the formal dedication ceremony. We had heard that national news media, like *U.S. News & World Report*, would be covering our unprecedented event. However, President Nixon had chosen that day, August 9, 1974, to resign from office. I don't have to tell you what took priority with the news media coverage that fateful day.

Nevertheless, it was a beautiful day. The ribbon-cutting ceremony took place outdoors with much fanfare. Seeing Joe's bigger-than-life photo staring at me was ... well, wonderful. I imagined him pleased. San Mateo dignitaries, General Cushman with his aides, and city citizens lined up to take the library elevator to the

Ribbon-cutting ceremony for the
Screaming Eagle Memorial Room

third floor. When the doors to the Screaming Eagles Memorial Room opened, visitors were greeted with a recording by the Hollies:

> *"The road is long,*
> *With many a winding turn,*

That leads us to who knows where
Who knows when.
But I'm strong,
Strong enough to carry him.
He ain't heavy, he's my brother.
So on we go.
His welfare is of my concern.
No burden is he to bear.
We'll get there.
For I know,
He would not encumber me,
He ain't heavy, he's my brother."

Joe's military portrait displayed alongside his 1967 letter to Linda

I thanked our Screaming Eagles Memorial Committee for the heart and soul and countless meetings they poured into this sacred project and, at the closing of the day, I left the room, unsure when I'd ever come back.

Reader, it may be hard to understand why I had to leave that special place behind, when I had worked so long and so hard for this day to come. But I could not face that room again until several years later. While it made me happy working on it, it also broke my heart at the same time. To keep entering that room and to, again and again, feel the solemn affect it had on me was simply too difficult to endure. Many Vietnam Veterans and their families report a similar type of overwhelming emotional response when visiting "THE WALL" in Washington for the first time. It can take all the strength you have. The Screaming Eagles Memorial Room was, and is, San Mateo's "WALL"... with memories, and names, never to be forgotten.

Chapter 14

These Boots Were Made for Walkin'[37]

"In the thick of it, we never had the opportunity to mourn for our losses. It was always on to the next trail, the next hill, or what could be just moments away ... the next firefight. And so, we grieve for them the rest of our lives."

— Anonymous 101st Airborne Paratrooper

"Silence ... the cannons no longer roar ... the machine guns are mute ... no longer do the sounds of bugles, whistles, and the cries of young men echo through a long-forgotten valley. However, the silence of our friends ... is deafening."

— Bryan Smothers, Vietnam Veteran, Author of *1968: Year of the Monkey*

I didn't serve or fight in Vietnam, but I do understand that sometimes the memories are too hard to bear. So despite having worked so hard on the memorial room, I had to walk away ... at least from that part of our mission. And at least for a while.

It was a long time — years — before I was able visit the room again. The only way to enter "The Room" was to take the library's elevator up, all the while knowing where that elevator would take me. The third floor. As the elevator door opened, Joe's face met me as I stepped out of the elevator. His portrait, and beside him his letter, "Sis, can you do me a favor ..."

Did I know it would be the last favor I ever did for my little brother? Gazing at his picture — at him — I remembered that last day we had together, not saying goodbye when he left for Vietnam, but the day he came back to us ... Standing there facing Joe's picture under the most heartbreaking of conditions, I see myself getting out of the car at Golden Gate National Cemetery, that cold day with crowds of people standing around, wearing solemn expressions. I stepped out of the car, forcing every step toward the Chapel where you laid, Joe. I couldn't make those steps without help, without someone holding my arm and pulling me forward to where you rested in your eternal sleep, little brother. I remember that just before I walked into that cold chapel, I grabbed a pillar in the entrance. *"NO GOD, I can't say goodbye this way ... Please don't make me ..."* Nearly five years later, that is what that room at the library did to me too. I knew what to expect the minute that elevator door opened. I couldn't revisit it — it hurt too much.

I asked myself, *"Would time heal this for me?"* I had nothing but time.

Flashing

I never physically humped any jungle trails or fought my way to the top of a muddy hill. I never had to watch a buddy bleed out or caress a dying child in my arms. But mentally I did. Through the letters I read — day in and day out for so many years — I experienced these things and more. As I read each letter that went into the Screaming

Eagles Memorial Room, it was as if Joe were writing, letting me know his feelings and taking me to a place that was forbidden to most. But could I really understand? I tried. I thought so many times, *"I'm there with you, dear brother."* Some days I walked around in a daze, and I thought about when we were kids. Had I done what Mom told me? "Linda you're the oldest; you are responsible for your brothers. Never forget that!" It seemed as if those words echoed in my brain. Did I let him down? Had I failed Joe?

Some things are best kept locked up and buried. But you can't put on enough locks. You can never bury them deeply enough. They break free with an odor. They unearth at the sound of the blades of a helicopter (and, believe it or not, a Huey's rotors is a sound I know well). A faded photograph opens an unwanted door. A Screaming Eagle challenge coin or a set of tarnished jump wings emerge from my treasured jewelry box while I'm looking for the right pair of earrings to wear. A song can take me instantly back there. It's like I'm in a time capsule where I remember every corner, the red dirt, the sugar cane given to me by some Vietnamese child. But most of all, it's the smiles on young people in the street here at home — today — that take me back to the faces of the young paratroopers I'd met. So many reminders were taking me back so often that people would notice the distant look in my eyes and say, "Hello, Earth to Linda, where are you?" I was there. In Vietnam.

The Daily Rosters that I received from the 327th while working on the Adopted Sons project were heartbreaking. It was soul wrenching when I saw the name of a paratrooper crossed out with a handwritten "KIA" next to it. It was especially crushing when I recognized the names of Soldiers who I had met while I was in Vietnam. One name that hit me particularly hard, and then again even more so when I learned the details of his death, was the 17-year-old who had turned 18 that Christmas week of 1968. You will recall I wrote about him in Chapter 7. I'm told that God has a plan for us all. I'm positive that

I was meant to be there as a witness to that young man's life — to meet that precious young boy with the flawless baby face and sparkling green eyes, to see the child, with all his might, blow out the candles on his birthday cake, and to hear the glee in his voice when he jokingly spoke of how he was now legally old enough to go on a combat patrol. His name was William B. Reedy. I was later told that, several months after that birthday celebration, while in the bush, he had stepped on a Bouncing Betty land mine. It did what it was designed to do. It popped up waist high and detonated. His young body was severed in two.

Chapter 15

Moving On ...
I Got Those Wedding
Bell Blues[38]

The war was over. The troops were home. The Memorial Room had been completed. Now it was time for Steve and me to plan our lives and future together.

If only life was that simple.

We set our wedding date for November 27, 1976. We had met in Vietnam and fell in love. Now it doesn't take new math to calculate that we were engaged for almost eight years. What couple do you know who've been engaged for eight years?

Why? Like everything else in my life, it's complicated. Steve had told me, within a month of our meeting, that he wanted to marry and spend the rest of his life with me. I was ready, willing, and able. There were only a few wee obstacles in our way in the beginning of our relationship, such as the fact that I had two children from a previous marriage and was living in California, whereas Steve's roots were in New York. Looking back, it was a lot to ask of a young man — to step into and take on the responsibility of a readymade family, all while reacclimating to civilian life after the horrors of war.

He assured me, every step of the way, that he wanted to build a future for us first and, if you know Steve, you know how methodical he is. His plans before meeting me were to go on to graduate school after the Army. However, our love put a damper on that, so he decided to complete training on Wall Street. He would work on earning his Series 7 licenses and become a stockbroker with a prestigious brokerage firm. Our separation would be brief during his training in New York. In the meantime, I would return to San Mateo and jump back into leading our Soldier adoption campaign. Through countless letters and phone calls, we tried to fill the gap of not being together. Steve would always tell me to "Keep the faith, Linda," and I did. Steve packed up everything, lined up a terrific job with a great investment firm in San Francisco called "Glore Forgan, Staats" and found an apartment to be close to me in San Mateo. Those were the years of the Women's Liberation Movement and, as such, living together before taking vows was not frowned upon but even encouraged. But that was not for us. Steve was raised with a strong Catholic background, I had two small children, and — against the norm of the times — we felt it just wasn't right to live together. Steve wanted it that way, so it was okay with me.

I had landed a great job with the California Teachers Association (CTA), working as a legal secretary for the lead General Counsel, and stayed with them for seven years We were married in San Mateo at St. Matthews Catholic Church, given permission by the priest because they didn't recognize my first marriage in Reno, which was officiated by a justice of the peace. I was so happy, feeling like this was my true marriage We had a small, intimate wedding with family and guests from CTA on November 27, 1976. Two years later, our son Stephen was born on November 23, 1978. Steve suggested I get my California real estate license. A career as a realtor can be relatively flexible, and this would allow me more free time to raise our new baby. I knocked myself out studying for the test and, to Steve's and my amazement, I passed. Apparently, I had a few smarts after all! Life was good. We bought our first home in Foster City. Craig and Destiny, my two oldest children, were 19 and 18 years old, adored their baby brother Stephen and were on their way to building their own lives. Craig headed to community college and a job at Mills Hospital in Burlingame, and Destiny found her niche as a stand-up comic in San Francisco. I was an empty-nester and a new mother all at the same time. Having a new baby and a new husband was a bit of like starting all over again. And it was as it should be ... a dream come true.

The Sounds of Silence[39]

The American involvement in the Vietnam War had been over for years, yet news articles would pop up from time to time about our Vietnam Veterans. Typically, and sadly, it was all negative. I felt anger while reading those articles. I hadn't forgotten how our Veterans were treated when they returned home, and I never will — EVER! I wished that during those turbulent times, I had been able to do more. A day never passed that I didn't think of our Vietnam Veterans. Steve and I moved on together, enjoying the nice ties of family life ... but the war was the loop that connected us. We shoved Vietnam back in memory, but it would surface many times in our daily thoughts and it would not easily fade. A mixture of pain and happiness.

How were our guys — our Screaming Eagles and all Vietnam Veterans — doing? Were they able to get on with their lives? Were they still suffering from the war? How did they feel about their Country just wanting to forget the war? To forget the men who fought and died ... never! Why did it take so long to honor them with The Vietnam Veterans Memorial Wall in Washington, D.C., in 1982? When it really meant something, why were they denied the respect they deserved?

I would forever ask myself these questions and refuse to accept the answers that were offered. Yet we moved on.

Same Mud, Same Blood*

In 1981, San Mateo, being the City that it was, under Mayor Jack Murray, decided to recognize ALL Vietnam Veterans with a City commemoration for their 101st Airborne. Fort Campbell, Kentucky, sent out a large contingent of Soldiers once again and the event was a wonderful tribute with a huge turnout. Troops parachuted from military planes right into Bay Meadows Racetrack. I remember Vietnam Veterans walking over to me and saying, with tears in their eyes, that this was their "Welcome Home." They were not part of San Mateo's Adopted Sons, but they felt like they were that day. HOOAH to Mayor Jack Murray that day!

Time, as people say, flew by. Before we knew it, it would be the 20th anniversary of the City's adoption of ABU/Assassins 1-327th Infantry, 1st Brigade, 101st Airborne. One of the medics in the unit, Doc Tavitian from Whitehouse, Ohio, made contact with Steve and suggested they hold their first formal reunion back in the City they remembered really cared, San Mateo. So together Doc, Steve and I began planning the first reunion for our adopted sons along with Jack Murray, who had rotated onto the City Council. Whatever the City could do for our ABUs, they would. As for Steve, he was ready to reconnect with his own men again, saying he was "proud beyond words to have served with these exceptional men of courage." And I was so excited! I could hardly wait to see them once again, at least the few who could make it to the reunion. We were, after all, not kids anymore and it had been a long time since 1968!

---

* "Same Mud, Same Blood" NBC News, New York, NY: NBC Universal, 12/01/1967. Accessed Fri Jan 10 2020 from NBC Learn: https://archives. nbclearn.com/portal/site/k-12/browse/?cuecard=72264

The date was set for our ABU reunion, July 1989 in San Mateo. The hotel would be the Holiday Inn in Foster City, a neighboring City to San Mateo and the town in which I lived with my family. Doc had done a fantastic job of alerting the troops and we had a nice turnout of approximately 50 Veterans — our adopted sons. San Mateo Mayor Jack Murray would ensure that the men had the red carpet treatment from their "adopted home" once again. Steve was the Master of Ceremonies and we kept speeches at the dinner to a minimum. What was most important was that the men were seeing each other again. I don't know if anyone on the outside could understand the importance each held for the other — the palpable and enduring brotherly love that was always with them. Few others had experienced what they shared fighting together. "Same Mud, Same Blood." Those who made it through hell would never have imagined that that hell would shadow their lives forever. But, even if only for a moment, the emotional rays of light were overpowering when they saw each other for the first time again. The sight of men bursting into tears and hugs was so heartwarming and rewarding. Maybe their faces and bodies were 20 years older, but their eyes still shined as 19 – and 20-year-olds. Once again, the brothers-in-arms were able to wrap their arms around one another and embrace as if they had never let each other go...

> **What was most important was that the men were seeing each other again. I don't know if anyone on the outside could understand the importance each held for the other — the palpable and enduring brotherly love that was always with them.**

My seeing them again released a flood of feelings that had long been bottled up. I let the feelings come rushing to the surface. They were, after all, my brothers too and I understood.

Chapter 16

What the World Needs Now Is Love[40]

It was the '80s and life was good. Steve had a great job and was at the peak of his career and we were about to break ground for a new house on sizable lot in prestigious Hillsborough, a bordering city to San Mateo. Our son Stephen, III, was in a great private school, just turning eight and I was selling homes, loving my job. Craig met a lovely girl and got married. Destiny was living in San Francisco and loving the adventure of the big city. Craig and Destiny came home often for dinner. Then Steve said, "Linda, we have a great opportunity, but it will mean moving to Los Angeles." Oh my god, WHAT? I never wanted to leave San Mateo but, I have to confess, once we visited La La Land, and particularly Pacific Palisades, I couldn't deny that it was beautiful. So near to the beach, with warm weather and sunshine and, gosh I guess being neighbors to Chevy Chase, kind of threw me off course. Exciting! Would I be selling houses to movie stars? Hmmmmmmmmmm.

OK, I broke down. In 1986, we bought a beautiful house in Pacific Palisades. I know you've heard of it from the Beach Boys. I even got to take one of the Beach Boys' wives (I think number 5) out to show houses to!! I've got to admit, it was fun while it lasted.

Then, suddenly in 1991, President George H. W. Bush announced we were at war again. Desert Shield, Desert Storm. One Vietnam friend, Tom Carhart — who was a lieutenant like Steve — had served and reconnected later with Steve. Tom called and said, "Linda, you should do what you did in San Mateo for our 101st troops preparing to deploy and fight." Tom promised he would help me get started.

Tom lived in Virginia and was a well-known author of military books. He took a letter over to the House of Representatives, explaining what I had done during the Vietnam War and said, "This lady is prepared to lead a nonprofit, calling it AMERICA SUPPORTING AMERICANS — ASA. Her mission is to bring American cities to 'adopt units' like she did during the Vietnam war." And so it came to be.

With Carhart's help, we formed a Board of Directors and, suddenly, Senators, Congressman and other political leaders were writing to their community leaders (like mayors), encouraging them to bring their cities to me. Now keep in mind, there were no email addresses or social media at the time. To communicate, ASA relied on snail mail and faxes. My real estate office was getting calls from across the country — Florida, Georgia, Texas, Virginia — with people leaving me messages, when my manager came to me and said, "Linda, now I know these people are not all wanting houses in the Palisades ... What's up?" Well, I confessed, I was getting involved with something that meant more to me than real estate. He smiled, but said, "Your paycheck will reflect it ... you're on commission." He let me do my own thing, selling houses and serving the troops.

Now my time was being consumed by the 101st and they were my top priority. The Battalion Commander, knowing my history, enlisted all his units with ASA Adopt a Unit.

This time, it came easier. Towns were answering me with "How do we adopt a unit?" Perhaps civic and municipal leaders, teachers and others were feeling a bit of guilt for how they treated our Vietnam Vets two decades ago. The sentiment had shifted. It seemed the nation was ready to never again turn their backs on our Soldiers, marines, sailors, airmen and coast guard.

Steve took a different look at all this, "Why again Linda?"

"Steve, it is something I have to do."

"You are spending too much time on this. It's not what I want for our family."

"But Steve, you must understand, you ... of all people."

Our attempts to persuade one another to see the other side simply didn't work. As such, there was tension in our marriage. When it came to war, he didn't want to be reminded and I couldn't let go.

> ## When it came to war, he didn't want to be reminded and I couldn't let go.

Then he told me burning words that pierced my heart. "Linda ... a war brought us together and a war will separate us." It's ironic, isn't it?

Those weeks were tearing us apart. But, thank God, we survived it. Love maintained us and reminded us of what we already knew: we lived for each other. Nothing would destroy our love ... not even another war.

Chapter 17

Where Were You When the World Stopped Turning?[41]

Early in the morning on September 11, 2001, Steve and I get a phone call from my daughter Destiny: "Mom, turn on your TV quick!!" Immediately, I turned the set on and looked at Steve. "Oh my god ... is this really happening ..." I said in disbelief. We were watching in real time as Americans were attacked on our own soil by terrorists who had hijacked four commercial airplanes. They were flying those planes into the World Trade Center's Twin Towers in New York, into the Pentagon, and into a field in Pennsylvania. Shock is the only word I can summon up to describe it. Both of us stood there in shock with the rest of the country, glued to our television sets and not knowing what to think or feel. We were listening to what our President, George W. Bush, would say next. And so it happened that America declared WAR against an enemy called al-Qaeda with a leader who called himself Osama bin Laden.

Steve and I knew what this would mean to America and our troops. Unfortunately, we can't all pick up a weapon, but I told Steve — and

this time I had his total support — "I'm bringing ASA to the fore-
front. Our troops will need our support." That day, I pulled out of my
closet the jungle fatigue jacket that was given to me in Vietnam, and
I put it back on. Later that day, I drove to our local coffee shop and,
while waiting in line, I felt a tap on my shoulder. I turned around
and a gentleman asked, "Miss, where did you get that jacket"? I told
him I got it in Vietnam. He next asked, "What were you doing in
Vietnam?" I grabbed my cup of coffee and he asked if we could
sit and talk.

He had been in Vietnam too. Turns out, he was attached to the 101st
Airborne. We introduced ourselves — his name was Joe Spooner,
he also lived in the Palisades and he was a neurologist. While in
Vietnam, he was with a PSYOPs (Psychological Operations) Unit.
We probably spent a good two hours talking in that coffee shop,
ending with him saying, "What can I do to help you with your organization? Let me know." I did. "Joe, I am reactivating ASA and I need
a treasurer." He answered right there on the spot: "I'm IN, Linda!" It
was not lost on me that, all these years later, as our nation was mired
in the emotions of a terrorist attack and a war in the Middle East, one
of the first people to appear in my life to help was a man named Joe.

And there were so many people who stepped up. It seemed like
everyone wanted to help! Tom Carhart, who helped me incorporate
ASA during Desert Storm, became our Chairman of the Board. Alan
Clark, an SEC Attorney with Latham & Watkins International Law
Firm, located in downtown Los Angeles, also became a member of
the new Board of Directors. Alan had been with me from the beginning of incorporating ASA in 1991. Julius Johnson, who was the
unit Company Commander for our first adopted unit in Vietnam
(my brother and husband's CO, now retired as a Brigadier General)
returned to ASA as a Board member finally. And Dr. Joseph (Joe)
Spooner became our Treasurer. ASA got to work.

Our first troops to contact were the Rakkasans, the 187th out of Fort Campbell, Kentucky, home base for the 101st Airborne Division "Air Assault." They were the first to deploy to Afghanistan to hunt for bin Laden and his al-Qaeda terrorist group.

ASA now became part of the computer social media age. We developed a website. This is where we met a very active lady whose dad was in WWII and her passion was helping Vets. Her name was Ginger Mozzetti, she had website and IT skills, and she developed a website for ASA — nothing fancy, but doable for our mission. Units and their families took notice of us and began to log on to our site, asking for us to find a city to "adopt their unit." Others — businesses, schools, athletic teams, church groups, civic leaders — heard about ASA by word of mouth and also requested if they could support a unit. ASA would refer to these non-city volunteers as "fostering a unit." This meant that we would assign a unit, usually a Company size of 130 Soldiers who were deployed. This would be considered a year-long "fostering" commitment of sending letters and care packages to the members of their unit. Our primary mission was to enlist cities and towns to formally "adopt" a unit. This would be an official action through the city or town's mayor and city council passing a resolution formally adopting a unit ASA assigned. Adoption was a long-term commitment. Our mission statement laid out our program.

As ASA began to grow on a global basis, it appeared that ASA needed a more professional website, at least according to our Board of Directors. Tom had known Ross Perot, and we all know that Mr. Perot was a passionate supporter of our Vietnam troops and our missing in action (MIA) Soldiers. Tom told him my story of Vietnam and Mr. Perot said he would be happy to help ASA. It was Mr. Perot who was able to get ASA on the Larry King Live show in 2004. Wow — the influence of a major network does wonders. I only had a 20-minute interview with Larry King, but our site had more than 20,000 visits in that 20-minute segment. Our site couldn't handle it. Or I should say,

MISSION

Adopt-a-Unit Program

The centerpiece of ASA's work is the Adopt-A-Unit Program. Believing that a strong, supportive connection between young men and women of our armed forces and the civilian communities they are ready and willing to serve is crucial to morale, ASA has committed itself to building and strengthening this link.

By coordinating with both civic and community groups, ASA facilitates "adoptions" between towns, cities, or counties and individual military units throughout the country. We work with all branches of the armed forces, including the National Guard, establishing adoptions between communities and units already interested in forming a partnership and between communities and units that have no previous connection with each other. In some cases, a city is already "home" to a particular unit, and the municipality and unit may want to solidify this relationship in unique, personally meaningful ways. In other cases, a city or town wants to establish a strong, supportive connection with Soldiers, Sailors, Airmen, Marines or Coast Guardsmen in a unit not already affiliated with the community involved. Both these situations result in rewarding, successful adoptions that are beneficial to everyone involved.

I couldn't handle the requests coming in from all across the country. I did, however, follow up with as many people as I could, resulting in enlisting several cities in Kentucky for our units. And because the 101st (Screaming Eagles) home base is located in Fort Campbell,

Foster-a-Unit Program

The ASA Foster-a-Unit Program provides the opportunity for businesses and organizations not involved in the Adopt-a-Unit Program to support the morale of troops serving in military units both at home and overseas while they wait for adoption through the ASA Adopt-a-Unit Program. A business, community group or school group not involved with local adoption activities can foster a military unit by sending one or two rounds of letters and/ or care packages to troops who are serving in harm's way.

Youth Civic Action and Awareness Program (YCAP)

ASA encourages adoptive communities to use their adoption programs to expand young people's understanding of America's role in global affairs, of the role the military plays in the American political system, and of the experience of American servicemen and women. With this in mind, YCAP enables teachers to use their community's participation in the Adopt-a-Unit Program to enrich their curricula and to add new dimensions to the learning that goes on in their classrooms.

Kentucky, these local connections were meaningful for Soldiers and civilians alike.

After watching my interview on the Larry King Show, one councilmember from Alexandra, Kentucky, John Stein, wanted to do more than just enroll his town of Alexandria. So he promoted ASA to other northern Kentucky cities, and the snowball began across the State of Kentucky State. Thanks to John Stein, several units with the 101st became "adopted" by Kentucky cities. John Stein arranged town hall meetings with Northern Kentucky cities where I attended. I witnessed an uncanny level of civilian patriotism from many of these communities. *"Would the South rise again, only this time for our troops and their families?"* I asked myself. This outpouring of support would catch on like a super charge for ASA.

Veteran support, as it turned out, was catching on everywhere. The President of the United States at the time, George W. Bush, created a homeland support program called "Support Our Troops" and his administration rounded up a few of us. I was honored to participate. My trip to the White House was in June 2005. There were about seven other troop support group leaders, including actor Gary Sinise who had starred in the blockbuster movie *Forrest Gump* as a Soldier wounded in Vietnam. We met in the Roosevelt Room of the White House and had an hour conversation with President Bush. The President asked us questions about our organizations, he encouraged us to continue and thanked us for our dedication and support for our troops. What an honor that was for us all! It was evident that this President realized the value of home support to our deployed service men and women, and he wanted Americans to actively take part in a "Call to Action." President Bush loved our military men and women.

I went back home with a clear understanding of ASA's role and realizing this war would not be fought like other wars. This enemy was cowardly and evil, more afraid of facing our troops. This battle would be a tough fight due to the enemy choice of weapons hidden — improved explosive devices (IEDs) capable of maiming and killing many of our Soldiers. Suicide bombers had no regard for life, including their own. And terrorists realized that they could not beat our troops on the battlefield. ASA felt that with each bomb, it was the will and resolve of the American people that was being attacked. ASA efforts and goals would be to focus on strengthening our nation's will and, with that, sustaining the morale of our brave troops.

With new cities logging on to our global website, enlisting their communities' support for every unit that came to us, it was apparent Americans cared. They just needed to understand how they could reach our troops and their families. Thousands of care packages were sent to Iraq and Afghanistan. However, it was ASA that developed sustaining relationships with their units, a unique part of our mission. Much is owed to cities like San Mateo, Burlingame and Hillsborough, and leaders like Norma Gomez, the City Clerk for years who reunited San Mateo once again after Desert Storm. Norma passed the torch on to Patrice Olds, San Mateo City Clerk, when Norma retired. Patrice ran with that torch. Let me say that again ... Patrice did not walk, she ran and raised it high! She made every new Commander at the 101st Airborne Division aware that her City would always stand by their "Adopted Unit."

Another Meaningful Reunion

Our work continued with vigor. And in our memories were always those original ABUs from Vietnam. In 2012, the City Clerk in San Mateo, Patrice Olds, coordinated her City's 40th Anniversary of the original 1972 San Mateo Vietnam Homecoming. The Brigade Commander, Colonel Thousands of care packages were sent to Iraq and Afghanistan; however, it was ASA that developed sustaining relationships with their units as it had during the Vietnam War. JP McGee brought his troops out from Fort Campbell, Kentucky, to commemorate the three-day event San Mateo was planning along with their neighbors, Burlingame and Hillsborough. Of course, ASA had a big role in this planning and was able to reach out to several of San Mateo's Vietnam Veterans, the Soldiers who were our "adopted sons" during the Vietnam War. Those three days in San Mateo where truly special. All in attendance were amazed, especially our Soldiers from the past and present. On the second day of the visit, our Veterans marched down the streets of San Mateo with Colonel McGee's young Screaming Eagles — a band of brothers across multiple generations. San Mateo's first "adopted sons," the original troopers, marched to the sound of a cheering crowd, breaking their parade progress only to shake a hand of a child watching, waving his or her little American flag at them. These Soldiers as they passed by were not slowed down by age but were in their minds 19 – and 20-year-old Soldiers again. The three-day 40th anniversary celebration was documented with a video called "The City with a Heart."

It's not easy to put into words the love and admiration that was felt by this town of 120,000+ for their Soldiers, past and present. Neither is it possible to adequately articulate the love and gratitude the Soldiers felt for the people of this City. After the parade, there were brief speeches of welcome and

50th Anniversary; ABU's original adopted sons at Joe's gravesite in Golden Gate National Cemetery, reading names of the brothers they lost, March 25, 2018

then, as had become tradition, a barbeque in San Mateo's Central Park. Everyone seemed to be taking pictures commemorating the day. There were dinners and hugs and conversations. The experience ended with Colonel McGee's troops and our Vietnam Vets attending a public memorial ceremony at Golden Gate National Cemetery, where my brother Joe had been laid to rest. Colonel McGee and his Soldiers and, of course, Joe's Vietnam brothers who fought alongside of him all came together to pay their respects. I simply knelt down and told him, "Joe, they are here for you, little brother." I kissed his headstone.

So Many Volunteers

With all the great support for ASA's units, there are countless volunteers who throw their hearts and souls into supporting their Soldiers. Great ASA leadership and compassionate men and women are found in towns like Villa Hills, Kentucky. Julie Schuler of Villa Hills has gone beyond what any one person could be expected to do, leading and partnering with Janie Terrill and Libby Graham Baker; these ladies our angels to their Soldiers and their families. Others, city leaders, their Mayors, their neighboring cities, Crescent Springs, Lakeside Park, Erlanger, joined at the hip to support an entire Battalion. The unique bond that has developed between every Change of Commander has strengthened the ties and their Soldiers' love these cities. The cities adopted battery units with the 2nd Brigade, 101st "TOP GUNS." It's almost like an umbilical cord between mother and child — separated at birth but always connected. I could go on and on about these Northern Kentucky cities and the patriotism among their citizens, but that would take another book, folks!

Faye McDonald, another outstanding volunteer, came to ASA to encourage her own State of Tennessee. Faye's husband was a TOP SGT during the Vietnam War and was loved by his men. Faye knew too well how Vietnam Vets had often been mistreated or dismissed, and she wanted to see that that never happened again. Her support and contributions were many to ASA.

Many more great Americans who love our Soldiers and have connected directly with their unit families are busy keeping the relationships strong through numerous Changes of Commanders and through deployment after deployment. Union, Kentucky, and

Florence, Kentucky, have quickly bonded as tight as Soldiers bond with one another. Rest assured, there is no breaking that chain.

During these early years of redeveloping ASA, much credit goes to a young Marine, Major Demetrius Maxey. Maxey had experienced ASA's support with his own Marine unit, 2-4 Marines out of Camp Pendleton, California. Major Maxey developed a grand ACTION PLAN for ASA and when he retired from the Marine Corps became ASA's Operation Director for a short time, as he was a true patriot. After leaving the Marines, he joined ASA as a volunteer and contributed much in the way of advice and consulting — always an asset and a friend of ASA. A few years later, he wanted to get back into serving his country so he re-enlisted, always promoting ASA when he could.

ASA takes unique pride in seeing these connections develop, especially when they spark love and understanding among our youth and educational groups. There's something so special about our youth groups who learn about the troops and serving the nation through educational outreach. Many athletic teams and their coaches have enlisted their teams to foster a unit. This is particularly true of teams who play the Native American game of lacrosse. Ironically, lacrosse, as played by tribal members was originally a means to train their young warriors for war. Legendary and Hall of Fame coach Sid Jamieson, himself a Native American and also my husband Steve's former lacrosse coach at Bucknell University, coached for some 38 years at Bucknell. He brought the lacrosse community into ASA. Sid became an active member of our Board.

Today, more than 90 lacrosse teams throughout the country have sponsored our troops as a result of Sid. Bob Rhein, with his lacrosse team the York Knights in Pennsylvania, made it evident what it means to be selfless supporters. He used the unit they were sponsoring as a model for his players of what they must endure and sacrifice to be better players and better young people. Bob had his team players think outside of the box and learn a lesson they would never forget. He taught his kids that our Soldiers abide by a creed and seven values upon entering the service to country. He believed his kids could benefit and take with them a life-changing experience with ASA. Bob taught his team that we have a duty, just as the men and women who place themselves in harm's way do, to protect our homeland, our families and our free nation. Those Seven Values of our Army are qualities that should be as important to us as individuals as they are to our Soldiers.

> We have a duty, just as the men and women who place themselves in harm's way do, to protect our homeland, our families and our free nation.

The Seven Values of the Army:

1. Loyalty
2. Duty
3. Respect
4. Selfless Service
5. Honor
6. Integrity
7. Personal Courage

It's Been a Long Time Coming[42]

It took 48 years, but finally a monument was erected to honor the 792 fallen Soldiers of the 327th. The 327th Infantry Regiment Vietnam Memorial was finally becoming a reality.

The Brigade Commander of the 1st Brigade "Bastogne" 101st
Airborne Division Air Assault at Fort Campbell, Kentucky,
approached Steve and me. Interestingly, his name was Colonel Rob
Campbell (i.e., Colonel Campbell from Fort Campbell). He told us
it was about time they had a monument for all those fallen Soldiers
of the "Honor and Country Regiment" 327th from 1965 to 1972, who
made the supreme sacrifice during the Vietnam War. We could not
agree more.

Steve and I were honored to be a part of the leadership for this initia-
tive. There would be a small Memorial Committee of four: me, Steve,
LT COL Lou McDonald (Retired) and CSM (Command SGT Major)
Joseph Bossi (Retired). Yet another "Joe" coming into my life. Joe
Bossi said that ASA would be the nonprofit that donors could use to
be a memorial contributor for the perpetual monument.

With the help of Lou McDonald (Ret. LTC), who would gather the
names of the fallen, birthdates and dates killed, Steve came up with
the idea that anyone who chose to could donate $327.00 (Regiment
Number) would receive a beautiful plaque of their chosen Fallen
Hero. This plaque became the symbol of a tangible healing process
for so many of our Vietnam Vets. And so we began. ASA's website
allowed our Vets to feel that they would be a part of the monument
to their fallen brother and a testament to their love, which would
stand forever.

Steve worked together with the professional design team from Hunt
Memorials in Nashville, Tennessee, and subject to the final approval
of the Memorial Committee, we would begin to meet to review the
progress. The objective would be to create a monument honoring
every brave young Soldier who had given his life, listing the names
of the fallen on four pillars. The pillars would use the finest granite
imported from Africa and Georgia ... only the best for our brothers.

Beginning in August of 2015, when Steve made his first presentation at a 101st Convention in Tennessee to its 327th Regt., we were officially "on the road" to share this story and make the monument a reality. I travelled to Branson, Missouri, to a Vietnam Vets reunion and finally to the San Francisco Bay area — back to San Mateo — the first and only city to formally adopt a unit within this regiment. Together, Steve and I made our appeal to the Mayor and City Council in October. Weeks later, the City of San Mateo, California, approved a sizable donation toward the building of our monument. $10,100 was awarded to the funding of our 327th Infantry Regiment Vietnam Memorial Monument. Approximately 20% of their "Adopted Sons" who were among those to be honored by the Memorial.

The American Legion Post 283 in Pacific Palisades, California, made a contribution of $15,000 and the 327th Infantry Website contributed $5,000 with matching donors adding a total of $10,000. Frankly, many of those involved thought it would take several years to raise the $45,000 needed. But in just three months, more than $65,000 was raised. All other donations came from the men, family and friends. Now, resulting from a change of command, we began working with Brigade Commander COL Boyer and Bastogne Staff to finalize a date of unveiling. The date was set for September 9, 2016, and hundreds attended.

COL Boyer, who introduced Brigadier General Julius Johnson as the keynote speaker, opened the ceremony. General Johnson commanded ABU (A) Company, 1st Battalion, 327th Regt., 1st Brigade, 101st Airborne Division in '67/'68. He knew many of the young men whose names were engraved on this monument, some of whom were his own men. He spoke of a young SGT Joe Artavia, who suggested he could ask his sister to see if the folks back home in her city of San Mateo, California, would consider adopting his unit. At first, then-CPT Johnson said, "Are you kidding? Don't we get *enough* hate mail?" But then he reconsidered because young SGT Artavia told him his sister would do the right thing. When he wrote to her about it, he said it could go far to, "bring our morale up as high as the clouds, please try Sis." Joe, at 19, lived just long enough to read the local paper sent to him by his sister. SAN MATEO ADOPTS UNIT.

Unveiling the 327th Regiment Fallen Soldiers Memorial, guarded by FT Campbell Brigade Soldiers, FT Campbell, Kentucky, September 2016

The tears flowed when General Johnson concluded his speech. Our young Soldiers then unveiled the monument. Poised off to the side in a protective stance, COL Boyer signaled his men for the 21-Cannon Salute

while Taps was played. Yes, each of them, all those named on those four pillars, were remembered and always would be for future generations to know who real heroes were.

The base of the memorial reads: "In the thick of it, we never had the opportunity to mourn for our losses. It was always off to the next trail, the next hill or what could be just moments away, the next firefight. And so, we grieve for them for the rest of our lives."

Indeed. We grieve and we remember.

Back home, I sit at my computer, waiting for the next unit request: "Ma'am, can you get my unit adopted, please ...?"

Chapter 18
The Wind Beneath My Wings[43]

It's hard to believe that more than 50 years have passed. *"Joe, you've been in the shadows but always with me. Oh, how I've aged, but not you, little brother. You are still 19 years old."*

Fort Campbell, Kentucky, home to the 101st Airborne Division "Air Assault," is a place where ASA (America Supporting Americans) is well known, where our Adopt a Unit history is strong and where non-Veterans like me are treated like family. Their elite Division's history, reaching back to WWII, is continually written about and documented — the stories of astonishing men and women who have served, who have sacrificed and who accomplished remarkable missions are many and take us to a place in memory and imagination that is hard to fathom. Their Soldiering has been commended by Presidents and Generals. If you look, you will find countless books, movies and stories of bravery about the young Americans who gave of self for the love of their brothers in arms, for their country and in service to something even greater than themselves. *My* story is about honoring *their* stories. So I continue, and I will until my dying day.

More adoptions, more reunions, more healing, more honor, more gratitude for those who serve and have served.

In September 2017, I had the privilege and honor of accompanying exceptional women Patrice Olds (San Mateo City Clerk), Phyllis Diskin (Deputy City Clerk), LeAnn Thornton (Police Department Town of Hillsborough representative) and one of ASA's new "adopted city of Atherton, California" representatives, Detective Jason Bollendorf, to Fort Campbell. The purpose of the visit was to attend a Change of Command Ceremony. It was at this event and ceremony that, together, we would meet the new Commander for our Brigade. COL Boyer would be officially passing the Colors of the Bastogne Brigade to COL Derek Thomson.

After the ceremony, we had a private meeting to meet and explain to Commander, COL Thomson, our unique history for one of his units who became San Mateo's own "Adopted Sons" during the Vietnam War. We proudly told him that we would be facing the 50th anniversary of that binding relationship in March 2018. We also shared the history of the Bay Area Peninsula cities that had adopted units in his brigade through San Mateo's example. COL Thomson was taken aback and astonished at hearing our story, and the details of our unique support program. Never in his military career had he heard of such a bond between civilian and military populations, particularly during the Vietnam War.

Patrice, representing her city of San Mateo, came prepared. She spoke of having put together in 2012 the 40th anniversary of the unprecedented three-day homecoming for their adopted unit back in January 1972, when our ABUs were first stepping onto American soil again after battle. As history depicts, that celebration in 1972 was the only formal "Welcome Home" given to Vietnam Soldiers in America honoring a full Company size of combat Soldiers. The span of support had continued and now San Mateo would be looking to celebrate —in grand fashion — 50 years since the initial adoption in 1968. Patrice proudly explained that her city had never wavered in their support for the unit. She proceeded to ask COL Thomson if he would be willing to bring out 50 of his Soldiers for a truly special commemoration the following year in 2018, noting that her Mayor and community leaders were already busy planning. She proposed this would include many of the original Vietnam Veterans, their families and members of the unit they still supported — service members who were now under COL Thomson's command. Patrice said San Mateo would be planning a four-day celebration and would incorporate the eight other cities with adopted units from his brigade on the Peninsula.

I will never forget the Colonel's look of amazement and immediate response. "YES!" he said boldly. And he answered further with, "We will make this happen!"

Our meeting with COL Thomson was concluded with an enthusiastic "Let's set the date!!

All agreed to set the date for the anniversary celebration as March 22-25, 2018, to be held in the City of San Mateo. Because of the approaching holiday season, our work was cut out for us to complete the planning in approximately three months for a multi-day, multi-city series of events. But we knew we could do it!

Patrice, under the instructions of her City, set the ball in

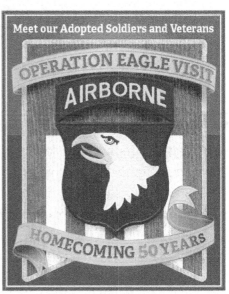

50th Anniversary Operation Eagles
Celebration, March 2018

motion. A planning committee was established and included repre-
sentatives of all nine cities: San Mateo, Hillsborough, Burlingame,
Foster City, Belmont, Atherton, San Carlos, Millbrae and San Bruno.
I would be in charge of notifying all original adopted sons, our
ABU Vietnam Vets. Alongside Steve, my husband and ABU platoon
leader, I would also serve on the fundraising committee and Vietnam
Veterans coordinating committee. We are talking about hosting well
over 100 active Soldiers, officers and Vietnam Vets and their families.
We could already feel the energy in the air.

With every committee meeting,
which they titled "Operation
Eagles Visit, II," ideas and
excitement grew — not only
on our end, but with word
reaching across the USA ...
filtering now to our Vietnam
Vets who had told their families, kids, grandkids and friends
how one city truly cared about
them. It seemed that history
would only tell of Vietnam
Vets who were shunned or
forgotten by their country. No

50th Anniversary Operation Eagles t-shirt
naming nine cities adopted by individual
units of Brigade all Cities, March 2018

parades or homecomings for them, at least not on a large scale. Only
San Mateo's "adopted sons" knew what it was like to be welcomed
home as an entire unit, celebrated as heroes and loved as sons and
brothers. For 50 years now, they had been showing off their precious
medallions, key to the city, cards, wallet gifts that had engraved
"Adopted Son." When they came home, they were embraced in every
way. Those memories they carried with them for 50 years.

We had not forgotten our original sons and they had not forgotten
us. We began to hear from them from across the country. Some had

health issues and traveling would be difficult, but we heard the same message over and over from Veterans and their families — they were going to make this trip "HOME," as they called San Mateo, come hell or high waters. Nothing would stop them. We heard stories about doctors not giving some

50th Anniversary parade with the flying eagle balloon

Veterans permission to travel. Those Veterans bought their airline tickets and fueled up their cars anyway. They were coming home again to the city that greeted them with open arms when they 18, 19 and 20 years, war torn, exhausted and unsure of what the future held. San Mateo would be where they would unite with their buddies, their brothers. Some had been to previous reunions; some had been to them all; some were coming back to see their friends for the first time in five decades.

As for our active young troopers who would be coming out from Fort Campbell, Kentucky, Patrice coordinated with COL Derek Thomson, and was told that the young Soldiers were excited to be able to meet the cities that had been supporting them in countless ways. COL Thomson directed that a contingent of Soldiers would attend the celebrations from each of the adopted units to further build on the relationships that were forming and thriving.

As expected, the four-day celebration was one for the ages. The days were so well planned by Patrice and her team of volunteers, too many to mention individually but they know who they are. Deep down, I know they know what patriots they are and how much their efforts

Young Soldiers from the 101st at the 50th Anniversary celebration

Veteran soldiers from the original 1968 adopted sons unit marching at the 50th Anniversary celebration

mattered. Every detail was attended to: hotel arrangements, days full of meaningful events, getting all the right community members on hand to create that sense of community our ABUs expected — adults and children, civic leaders, Veteran groups, firemen, police officers. So many people came out to celebrate, and they all wanted to see the troops they had come to respect, appreciate and love.

On Day One, there was a "Welcome Troops and Vets" celebration at San Francisco International Airport (bagpipers, signage and cheering crowds), a star-spangled escort to the hosting hotel and

The original ABUs at Golden Gate National Cemetery

several welcome events. On Day Two, we held a 'Sore' with the Eagles Workout in the morning before Soldiers met with their adopted cities and interacted with citizens. On Day Three, there was a parade in downtown San Mateo, a festival in Central Park and gala banquet. On Day Four, we enjoyed breakfast at a historical mansion and participated in a memorial observance at Golden Gate National Cemetery, where troops and Vets visited SGT Joseph Artavia's gravesite.

Until We Meet Again

At the time of the 50th anniversary celebration in 2018, I was writing this book, knowing it was time to share this story with the world. It was time to honor the tens of thousands of men and women in uniform — and their families — who allowed me and my colleagues to be part of *their* stories, even if only in a tiny way.

And here we are, at the end of the book, but surely not the end of this love story. Thank you to the civilian and military leaders who believed that a fearless (and perhaps naïve) young woman in a mini skirt could be an unofficial and meaningful ambassador to our troops in Vietnam. Thank you to every single man, woman and child who has written a letter, bestowed a hug, shed a tear or shopped for the contents of a care package headed to our service men and women deployed overseas. Every moment and every gesture has mattered.

> ## How do you end a story, close the page on a mission that has leaped mountains, crossed oceans, and loved and honored so many?

Do we say, "Goodbye?" How do you end a story, close the page on a mission that has leaped mountains, crossed oceans, and loved and honored so many? I love my God, my family and my Country. While I never officially raised my hand to take that oath of service that our uniformed men and women have, I have seen the good that is brought into our lives and our world by those who have. I see that goodness in every person who ever put on a uniform. And I have seen it especially in two men — my husband and my brother. My husband Steve is my personal hero, my personal Soldier ... the man who was and still is admired by so many who served with him and within his command. Some have said they trusted LT Patterson unconditionally and, if need be, would "march into hell" with him. I can see why. My brother Joe is my daily inspiration. I will be forever grateful for all the brothers he brought to me as he left this life, and indebted to my City of San Mateo, who stood as one, and to all the cities after. I am overwhelmed with love for my Soldiers, their families and the officers who guided me and the great Americans I met along the way, who joined me on this journey.

No goodbyes! No goodbyes to ASA or to my Screaming Eagles. Until my last breath ... I love you all!!

The Way They Were

ABU Soldiers

"Ask Not What Your Country
Can Do for You, but What You
Can Do for Your Country"
poster, *The Times*, June 1968

Jungle Hunt: CPT Julius Johnson and his radio-man (RTO) SPC4 Charles Bridgeman move along a jungle trail during Operation Klamath Falls; Johnson Commands ABU, January 1968

ABU Soldiers posing for Linda in Vietnam

Rick Smith, ABU, AKA "Wild Bill," wearing a full rucksack; this is what the average troop carried through the jungle

Eagles standing guard

Near Huế, Vietnam, April 1968; sister unit A Company,
2nd Battalion of the 327th Regiment, with SGT Baldwin
guiding a medevac chopper in to pick up the wounded

(Copyright Art Greenspon/Associated Press)

ASA, Still Going Strong

Troops and Civilian Connections

ASA and Desert Storm, 1991

ASA troops deployed in Iraq

Troops
unloading
mail

Troops
celebrating with
their care packages

Desert Storm, July 1991 homecoming in San Mateo; 1st Battalion, 327th Regiment, under the Command of LTC Hancock

ASA California City represents in Nashville, TN (October 2019); From left to right: COL Thomson, Maureen Freschet, Linda, Patrice Olds and LeAnn Thornton

2019 Iraq deployment of Soldiers from their home base in Alaska; fostered by numerous ASA sponsors

Clipping from Operation Desert Storm
homecoming, 1991

Artavia's grave site. The ceremony was held July 5 in San Bruno.

Lt. Col. Frank Hancock, commander, 1st Bn., 327th Inf. Rgt., enjoyed spending time with his desert pen pal Genevieve Mahrheinke.

Students reading letters
from the first Gulf War

United We Stand, 50th
Anniversary Celebration

Vietnam Veteran
medic Doc Tay and
Burlingame, CA, child

A gift to Steve and Linda from
ABU Vietnam Veteran Rene
Aries — a picture of ABU!

Gulf War 101st soldiers honor Joe,
the first adopted son, at Golden
Gate National Cemetery, 1991

Vietnam Adopted Sons and
101st Adopted Sons come
together from 1968 to 2018

Acknowledgments

In Memory of Bryan Smothers: A decorated Vietnam Veteran who served with the 101st Airborne Division and author of the book *1968: Year of the Monkey*. I met Bryan at a 101st Airborne Association Convention in 2015. Walking up to the table where he was selling copies of his book, I told him I was thinking of writing my own story of my Vietnam experience. I asked if I could contact him for any advice. Bryan, without any hesitation, said, "Yes. Let me know how I can help you." I asked, also, if I could buy a copy of his book. Bryan would not take any money from me but wrote a beautiful inscription in the book.

After reading Bryan's book, I knew he was the one I wanted to help me with mine. I owe Bryan a world of thanks for having inspired me and for always taking the time to read my chapters. He always told me, "Keep writing, Linda. Your story is unique and should be told." It was Bryan's idea to use songs of the '60s as chapter titles and subheadings. He reviewed my chapters one by one and offered advice and powerful perspectives. Bryan passed away before I could complete *A Dove Among Eagles*. I will never forget Bryan for all his support and I am so grateful to him. Without Bryan, this book would still be on a back burner and not in your hands. I know that Bryan is with Joe in heaven now.

To Jeffrey Knisely, a family relation to Bryan Smothers and a retired teacher who Bryan had used for his own story and then introduced to me. Jeff assisted in many ways — helping with everything from sentence structure to morale. Together with Bryan, Jeff encouraged me to keep writing. Thank you, Jeff, for ensuring this book got written.

To Joseph (Joe) Brazen, who I met with his beautiful actress wife Randi while searching for a home for them as their realtor in 1987. Joe was a screenwriter and director of a few short films and learned of my story. This was after the acclaimed film *Platoon* was released and Joe immediately expressed interest in the film rights to my story: "Linda, I want to write a screen play and your story should be made into a movie." After much initial brainstorming, we secured entertainment attorneys and moved forward. Joe had difficulty obtaining funding from the Hollywood moguls, though they did claim interest in my story. The script Joe wrote ultimately didn't go anywhere but remained titled "A Dove Among Eagles" — the title I loved. The project was dropped. Years later, when I started to write my book, I remembered Joe's title, searched and found him (in Washington State) and asked his permission to use the title, to which he owned the copyright. He responded, "Linda, it's yours to use. After all, it is *your* story." Thank you, Joe, for your belief and support so long ago and for giving me permission to use *A Dove Among Eagles ...* so fitting for my book.

To the City of San Mateo, California, and especially City Clerk Patrice Olds for her unbelievable support of encouragement, love of our troops, the history of her City's relationship and her amazing leadership in honoring our original adopted-son Vietnam Vets with two unprecedented, large-scale, multi-day events.

To Norma Gomez, San Mateo's previous City Clerk, who passed the torch to Patrice upon her retirement. Norma maintained her support for the troops, carrying on after the Vietnam War, making numerous trips to Fort Campbell, Kentucky, to meet new commanders of San Mateo's Adopted Sons (and now, daughters too!). Norma helped the city for Desert Storm troops returning to San Mateo to show their appreciation for all the support they received during the Gulf War.

Special acknowledgment to ASA Board members, past and present, our volunteers and our partners at America Supporting Americans. I am indebted to countless City Councils, Mayors, ASA representatives in so many States, athlete coaches, their teams (more than 90 lacrosse teams!). There are far too many people to thank individually, but you all know who you are. All of you are true patriots and are role models in the way you express your respect for our military men and women. I am inspired by your volunteerism, love of country and affection for the men and women who serve and sacrifice for all of us. This book is written because of you.

To the Officers, Commanders, and Military leaders I have known, up close and from afar. Where, how and why would *A Dove Among Eagles* be without your 50+ years of acknowledging the impact ASA has made on your Soldiers, Marines, Sailors, Airmen, National Guardsmen and their families? Through years of change of command and briefing new commands to carry on with ASA and their support for your Companies, Battalions, Brigades, Ships and Squadrons, the impact of our collaboration was never lost. Through ASA and our relationships with you, the force is stronger at home during war and peace.

Thank you, Colonel Robert Campbell for all your encouraging words and support, and for leading me and my book to the front door of your publisher. Thank you for your early review of the book and for your heartfelt foreword. You are a treasure.

To the team at Silver Tree Publishing — Kate Colbert, Penny Tate, Courtney Hudson and others — for believing in my story, turning me into an author and inspiring me every step of the way.

To my endorsers — Libby Graham Baker, Bo Brabo, Rob Campbell, Maureen Freschet, Ben Hodges, Julius Johnson, Patrice Olds, Jim Reynolds, Julie Schuler, Rick Smith, Joseph Spooner, Nancy Taylor, Brandon Teague and Derek Thomson.

To my personal friends —There are so many of you who I want to thank, and I can't possibly list you here. But a special thanks to Jim Sumner, for believing in ASA, listening to my story and developing ASA's first chapter in Greater Conejo Valley. To LeAnn Thornton, Julie Schuler, Kim Voss and Kit Stewart Legato.

To my children, Craig, Destiny and Stephen. You are the very best parts of me. Thank you for sharing your mom with so many, and for understanding that I had love in my heart for our Veterans in addition to my deep, unconditional love for you.

To my brother Eddie. After reconnecting, we cried together. Ed, I know the pain you still carry for Joe, as you know he always looked after you. I know and understand how it is difficult today as you told me crying, "I miss Joe so much I don't know what to do. I want to talk with my brother, it is difficult for me sis ... I love him so much ..." Keep him close in your heart as I have. I know he came to you recently in your dreams; I believe it is Joey's way of reaching out to you, to us. After all, it took 40 years for you and me to come together again ... Who did that? Joe!!

To our Veterans. ABU, this is you!! You've touched the lives of so many. I am grateful beyond adequate words to generations of Soldiers and officers along this long and meaningful journey. Love guided us all.

And with the deepest part of my heart, I express my thanks to my husband Steve Patterson. He is the Soldier I fell in love with during that brief but lifechanging trip to Vietnam, where I realized against all odds the likelihood of meeting such a man. How could I not fall in love with him, after seeing his character and heart on full display and after hearing stories during my visit from his men? LT Steve Patterson was a Soldier's Soldier — one his men said they would march into hell for. The grunts speak the truth about their Commanders — the trust, faith, devotion and, yes, brotherly love they hold for their combat leaders. Steve was a platoon leader who loved his men and the men loved him. I love him too. I became the luckiest woman in the world when he asked me to be his wife and escort me 'til the end of time. It was our "Look of Love."[44]

And the Beat Goes On...

From a Memorial Day message on Facebook, posted May 27, 2019, by Paul Hernandez.

"Nothing could ever fill that place in your heart that only your brother Joe reigns. No amount of condolences would ever make up for how hard it was for you to walk through that time. I can feel the hurt, as you shared this with us ... You lost a brother, but you gained a thousand brothers. We could never make up for Joe, but believe me, we love you and appreciate everything you have done for us. We original brothers are getting fewer but know you are so special since the first time we met you that Christmas. If you had asked us each what we experienced when we saw you, we would each express feelings of home, parents, girlfriends, friends, mom's cooking ... something we all wanted to get back to if we survived our time there. You brought the best Christmas present we could ever want. We had never experienced anything like this so far from home. That feeling of wanting one more time to be with family at Christmas. That present was you. Thanks Sis, for sacrificing for us. I hope you have a little extra love for your original brothers of 1968. Love you."

Awards, Honors and Decorations

For their service to this nation, the three pivotal individuals in this book — Linda Patterson, Steve Patterson and Joe Artavia — have received many awards, honors and decorations.

Linda Patterson

Founder, America Supporting Americans

- Department of the Army, Outstanding Civilian Service Medal – 2005 and 2012

- Inducted as an Honorary Distinguished member of the 1-320th Field Artillery Regiment, 101st Airborne Division (Air Assault) – 2009

- Secretary of the Army, Public Service Award – 2009

- President's "Call to Service Award" from the President's Council on Service and Civic Participation – 2005

- The Eagle Service Award presented by General David Petraeus – 2004

- Inducted as an Honorary Member of the 327th Infantry Regiment, 101st Airborne Division (Air Assault) – 2004

- The City of Los Angeles Commendation Award – 1993

- Appointed "First Citizen" of the San Francisco Peninsula by the San Francisco Board of Supervisors – 1972

LT Steve Patterson

A Company, 1/327 Infantry Regiment, 1st Brigade, 101st Airborne Division

- The Silver Star

- The Bronze Star for Meritorious Service

- The Army Commendation Medal with "V" Device for Heroism (with one oak leaf cluster)

- The Purple Heart (with one oak leaf cluster)

- Air Medal

- Vietnam Service Medal with One Silver Service Star

- Republic of Vietnam Campaign Medal with Device

- Republic of Vietnam Gallantry Cross with Palm Unit Citation

- Republic of Vietnam Civic Actions Honor Medal First Class Unit Citation

- Armed Forces Expeditionary Medal

- Korea Defense Service Medal

- Combat Infantry Badge

- Parachutist Badge

- Ranger Tab

- Awards Received Post Active Duty

- Inducted into Massapequa, New York's "Hall of Fame" – 2017

- Recognized by the Sigma Chi Fraternity as a "Significant Sig" – 2014

- Inducted as a "Distinguished Member of the 327th Infantry Regiment, 101st Airborne Division" – 2013

- Bucknell University's Distinguished Service to Country Award – 2002

SGT Joseph Gregory Artavia

A Company, 1/327 Infantry Regiment, 1st Brigade, 101st Airborne Division

- The Silver Star

- The Purple Heart

- The National Defense Medal

- Vietnam Service Medal with One Bronze Service Star

- Republic of Vietnam Campaign Medal with Device

- Republic of Vietnam Gallantry Cross with Palm Unit Citation

- Combat Infantry Badge

- Sharpshooter Badge with Machine Gun Bar

- Parachutist Badge

Songs and Lyrics
The Music We Lived and Died By

A quick reference guide to the song titles and lyrics mentioned in this book. Like most iconic songs, many of these have been covered and remade countless times. Included here are simply the most popular renditions or those the author remembers most vividly.

1. "Papa Was a Rollin' Stone," The Temptations, 1972

2. "Town Without Pity," Gene Pitney, 1961

3. "The Impossible Dream (The Quest)," from the 1965 Broadway musical *Man of La Mancha*, then notably performed in the '60s by performers including Frank Sinatra, Andy Williams, Jim Nabors, The Temptations, Shirley Bassey and Glen Campbell

4. "Dream On," Aerosmith, 1973

5. "See You in September," The Happenings, 1966

6. "Rainy Days and Mondays," The Carpenters, 1971

7. "On Eagles' Wings," Christian Hymn

8. "Come Fly with Me," Frank Sinatra, 1958

9. "Do You Know the Way to San Jose," Dionne Warwick, 1968

10. "I'll Be Home for Christmas," Bing Crosby, 1943

11. Sly and the Family Stone rose to fame in the mid-1960s, with hits like "Dance to the Music" and "Everyday People"

12. "Oh My Darling, Clementine," notably performed by Jack Narz and by Jan and Dean, 1959

13. "I Heard the Bells on Christmas Day" is a Christmas carol based on the 1863 poem "Christmas Bells" by American poet Henry Wadsworth Longfellow, and is the source of the popular holiday wish, "peace on earth, good will to men"

14. "It Came Upon the Midnight Clear" is an 1849 poem and Christmas carol written by Edmund Sears

15. "Suzie Q," Creedence Clearwater Revival, 1968

16. "Land of 1000 Dances," Wilson Pickett, 1966

17. "Mustang Sally," Wilson Pickett, 1966

18. "The First Noel," a Christmas carol of Cornish origin, first published by William Sandys and Davies Gilbert in 1823

19. "Silent Night," a Christmas carol of Austrian origin, composed in 1818 by Franz Xaver Gruber to lyrics by Joseph Mohr

20. "The Song from Moulin Rouge (Where Is Your Heart)," from the 1952 film *Moulin Rouge*, with music by Georges Aurie and French lyrics by Jacques LaRue

21. "This Magic Moment," The Drifters, in 1960, with a notable rendition by Jay and the Americans in 1968

22. "All My Loving," The Beatles, 1963

23. "Turn the Page," Bob Seger, 1973

24. "Express Yourself," Charles Wright & the Watts 103rd Street Rhythm Band, 1970

25. "Ain't No Sunshine," Bill Withers, 1971

26. "Don't Rain on My Parade," Barbara Streisand, 1968

27. "The Times They Are a-Changin,'" Bob Dylan, 1964

28. "The Beat Goes On," Sonny & Cher, 1967

29. "Ball of Confusion," The Temptations, 1970

30. "War (What Is It Good For?)," Edwin Starr, 1970

31. "For What It's Worth," Buffalo Springfield, 1966

32. "Turn! Turn! Turn! (To Everything There Is a Season)," 1965

33. "Where Have All the Flowers Gone," Peter, Paul and Mary, 1967

34. "The Times They Are a-Changin,'" Bob Dylan, 1964

35. "We Gotta Get Out of This Place," The Animals, 1965

36. "He Ain't Heavy, He's My Brother," The Hollies, 1969

37. "These Boots Were Made for Walkin,'" Nancy Sinatra, 1966

38. "Wedding Bell Blues," The 5th Dimension, 1969

39. "The Sound of Silence," Simon and Garfunkel, 1966

40. "What the World Needs Now Is Love," Jackie DeShannon, 1965

41. "Where Were You When the World Stopped Turning?," Alan Jackson, 2002

42. "A Change is Gonna Come," Sam Cooke, 1964

43. "Wind Beneath My Wings," Bette Midler, 1988

44. "The Look of Love," Dusty Springfield, 1967

Go Beyond the Book

A Message from Linda About Keeping in Touch

Thank you for reading *A Dove Among Eagles*! For those of you who feel you would like to join our ASA (America Supporting Americans) Adopt-a-Unit support team, here are some suggestions for how to help us, help our troops and experience one of the most rewarding things you can do in your life.

Learn More or Adopt a Unit

Connect with ASA at www.ASA-USA.org and click "Get Involved" on our home page.

This will take you to a brief form so you can reach us. If you have a community interest or wish for us to reach out to your city/town/business/school/church, please tell us. ASA will explain the guidelines and get the ball rolling. Contacting us is the first step.

Learn more about what we do by reading the Mission Statement on our website or reviewing our program over in Chapter 17 of this book.

f   Follow us on Facebook!
www.Facebook.com/AmericaSupportingAmericans

Start a Conversation

in   www.LinkedIn.com/in/Linda-Patterson-39389748

f   www.Facebook.com/ADoveAmongEagles

✉   Artavia101@Earthlink.net

📞   Office phone: 310-459-5625

📞   Cell phone: 310-463-9634

Invite Me to Speak to Your Group

If you'd like for me to speak to any large group, I'm interested. I'd love to visit your Veterans organizations, military bases or troop-support events. My husband Steve manages requests for media appearances, interviews and speaking engagements. Find Steve on his cell phone at 310-804-4945.

I live in Southern California. We welcome everyone.

Don't Be a Stranger!

Our active military units will go to our ASA website for the sole purpose of reaching out to us on behalf of their servicemen and women, desiring of building a strong sustaining relationship with civilian communities. We look for Americans to answer their plea.

ASA is only one phone call or e-mail away. We look forward to meeting you! Thank you.

About the Author

Linda Patterson is the Founder and President of America Supporting Americans (ASA USA), a nonprofit organization that links active military units — across all branches of service, including the National Guard — with cities, towns and counties through an "adoption" program intended to raise the morale of those who serve while strengthening the communities of civilians who support them. Linda has enlisted more than 300 cities across the United

States to adopt Army, Navy, Marine and Air Force units stationed around the world. In 2018, Linda helped host a four-day celebration in San Mateo, CA, honoring the original "adopted sons" of the Army's 101st Airborne Division alongside those active units the City has continued to support. Linda's brother, SGT Joseph "Joe" Artavia, a paratrooper with infantry unit and famed "Bastogne Brigade" of the 101st Airborne Division (the Screaming Eagles), was killed in combat in Vietnam in March of 1968. For her unwavering love and support, his comrades still call her "Sis."

The moment she set foot in Vietnam — Christmas of 1968 — during wartime, with no government approval, Linda Patterson became a living legend with an ambitious mission. And for 50 years, she's proven that those of us at home can do much to raise the morale of our military's men and women so they can "soar as high as the clouds," as her brother Joe had written in his last letter. Without realizing it and by simply doing her best to honor her brother's memory, Linda has become a source of inspiration for many ... for women daring to dream, act and love fearlessly ... and a place of comfort and acknowledgment for our troops, military families, civilian volunteers and entire communities.

Linda is the proud recipient of many local, regional and national awards and honors, including the Army's Outstanding Civilian Service Award. She lives in Pacific Palisades, CA, with her husband Steve. *A Dove Among Eagles* is her first book.

SGT Joseph G. Artavia
California

Company A, 327th Infantry
101st Airborne Division
Vietnam

January 1, 1949 – March 24, 1968

Never Forgotten

Made in the USA
Middletown, DE
07 March 2020

85816766R00119